SPECIAL EatingW

Mediterranean Diet

A Delicious Path to Lifelong Health

Contents

Parts of this special edition were previously published by *EatingWell* and *Cooking Light*.

INTRODUCTION

A TIMELESS (AND TIMELY) WAY TO EAT

Long-term studies have shown that people who adhere to the Mediterranean diet and lifestyle have a lower risk of developing diseases like diabetes, tend to live longer and age with grace. Here's what eating and living like a Mediterranean means and how you can adopt these principles no matter where you live.

BY JOYCE HENDLEY

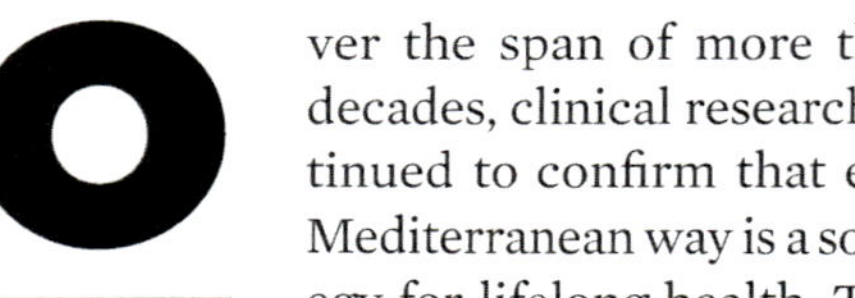ver the span of more than eight decades, clinical research has continued to confirm that eating the Mediterranean way is a sound strategy for lifelong health. The Mediterranean diet now routinely tops annual "best diet" roundups, and a "Healthy Mediterranean-Style Eating Pattern" is even called out in the 2015 edition of the U.S. Dietary Guidelines.

And no wonder! Unlike the sometimes dreary-sounding "prudent diets" or "healthful eating patterns" nutrition experts might recommend, the Mediterranean diet is what researchers might call "highly palatable"—i.e., delicious. Whether it's a platter of salmon cakes with arugula salad, or a hearty chicken and chickpea stew, Mediterranean dishes are a deliciously easy sell.

At its heart, though, the Mediterranean diet is precisely the way nutrition experts have been urging us to eat since, well, forever. It's built on a foundation of whole, mostly unprocessed foods like whole grains, beans and nuts. It embraces fruits and vegetables with abandon while being stingier with red meat and sweet treats. It includes moderate amounts of fish, eggs and dairy products, though vegan and vegetarian versions are eminently doable. It's sprinkled with heart-healthy vegetable oils—most famously, olive oil—rather than saturated-fat-rich butter or lard. And it can even include, if desired, a little alcohol—traditionally, red wine—enjoyed in moderation as part of a meal. What's not to love?

Modern research confirms ancient wisdom. Science continues to support the sensibility of this plant-forward eating pattern and the abundance of vitamins and minerals, antioxidants,

anti-inflammatory compounds, fiber and good fats it provides. Long-term studies have found that people who eat Mediterranean-style tend to have lower rates of heart disease and diabetes and a reduced risk of developing some cancers, including breast, prostate and colorectal cancer.

People who follow a Mediterranean diet also tend to live longer and perhaps age more gracefully: A recent meta-analysis of four studies involving elderly patients found that those who adhered most closely to a Mediterranean-style eating pattern had significantly less risk of becoming frail, an important measure of quality of life for older adults.

Encouraging research suggests that a Mediterranean pattern of eating may also have benefits for the brain. Several studies have linked the eating pattern to lower rates of depression; others note a small but significantly lower risk of developing mild cognitive impairment (MCI) and of MCI progressing to Alzheimer's disease. Also showing promise in several studies is the MIND diet (Mediterranean-DASH Intervention for Neurodegenerative Delay), a variation of the Mediterranean eating pattern that incorporates principles of the blood-pressure-lowering DASH diet (Dietary Approaches to Stop Hypertension). Rich in vegetables (especially green leafies), berries and fatty fish, the MIND diet may help slow age-related cognitive decline through the antioxidant and anti-inflammatory compounds those foods contain.

LUCKILY, YOU DON'T HAVE TO LIVE IN GREECE, ITALY or Tunis to enjoy a Mediterranean diet; it's a flexible eating pattern that allows endless interpretations. Build your meals around generous portions of vegetables and fruits, fresh and seasonal whenever possible. Consider the American Heart Association's recommendations for fruits and vegetables a good guide: 4 to 5 servings of each per day. While that sounds like a lot, a "serving" is just ½ cup (or 1 medium piece of fruit, or 1 cup of leafy vegetables). You could meet the goal by having fruit at breakfast, adding an extra serving or two of vegetables to your lunch and dinner and having prepped vegetables and fresh fruit on hand for snacking. And it's very Mediterranean to have some fresh fruit for dessert, perhaps with some nuts on the side.

Mediterranean cookbooks are filled with recipes made with beans, lentils, chickpeas and other legumes. They're a great source of high-quality protein and fiber—two ingredients that help make meals more satisfying; research suggests that if you're trying to lose weight, incorporating more legumes into your plan could make the journey a little easier. Getting more protein from plants and less from animal sources is a great way to reduce your carbon footprint too.

Trade up to whole-grain versions of breads, pastas and rice; nowadays they're easy to find on supermarket shelves. Experiment with some of the other whole grains widely used throughout the Mediterranean, like bulgur, farro, millet, whole-grain barley or couscous. You'll love their nuttier flavors and chewier textures, and you'll be getting more phytonutrients and fiber in every bite.

While your meals don't need to float in olive oil, it's a good idea to make it your go-to fat. Besides having a wonderful ability to make healthy foods (particularly vegetables) taste more delicious, olive oil is rich in monounsaturated fatty acids (MUFAs), known to help raise heart-friendly HDL cholesterol. Extra-virgin olive oil is also an extra-good source of oleocanthal, a phenolic compound known to have inflammation-fighting effects.

Other sources of heart-healthy MUFAs include canola, peanut and high-oleic safflower or sunflower oils, as well as avocados and nuts. But since fats and oils are rich in calories, it's important to keep an eye on portions, too; enjoy your olive oil in sprinkles, not glugs, and enjoy nuts by small handfuls, not cupfuls.

If you eat meat, think like a Mediterranean and enjoy it only occasionally, treating it more as a garnish than a main event (say, in a vegetable-rich stew or stir-fry) and lean more on fish, poultry, eggs and dairy. Aim to have fish and shellfish twice a week—including fatty types like tuna, sardines and salmon, which are rich in heart- and brain-friendly omega-3 fatty acids. Traditional Mediterranean diets also include some poultry, eggs and dairy products—usually yogurt and cheese. Evidence suggests that these fermented dairy products make the diet more nutritious and easier to stick with and that they don't appear to negatively affect cholesterol profiles when eaten in moderation. As sources of probiotic ("good") bacteria, they may also contribute to better gut health.

Consider sweets and sugary drinks "treats"—i.e., occasional indulgences. Mediterranean meals often end with a little fruit and/or cheese but rarely a sweet—and soda and other sugar-sweetened beverages aren't daily fare.

Mediterranean cooks often season with gusto and use healthy amounts of fresh herbs and spices as well as aromatics like garlic and onions. Not only do they make daily meals more interesting and tasty, but many have been found to have health-boosting effects, including fighting inflammation, lowering blood pressure and helping regulate blood sugar levels. To get more flavor into your meals, flex your palate and explore more dishes that use these seasonings abundantly—like the ones in these pages.

It's important to remember that the traditional Mediterranean way of life is an active one, with plenty of daily physical activity and social interactions with family and community. In the words of Spanish researcher Iglesias Lopez, its selection of healthy foods are "complemented by a philosophy of life that values personal relationships, the pursuit of happiness and physical activity."

This was borne out in a major study that followed 11,800 Spanish adults for 8½ years. It followed people who lived the Mediterranean way, combining a healthy eating pattern with staying physically and socially active. That group was 50% less likely to have depression by the study's end.

One last fact to ponder: Calling the Mediterranean way of eating a "diet" is something of a misnomer. What's abundantly clear, from centuries of practice and volumes of research, is that a Mediterranean diet is a lifestyle that's a pleasure to follow. Eating moderately and deliciously, being active daily, being involved with family and community—it's all part and parcel of what makes the Mediterranean way so beguiling. It's a prescription for a healthier, happier life by anyone's standards.

Ready to dig in? Turn the page. ●

CHAPTER 1

BETTER YOUR HEALTH

Research suggests that the benefits of following a Mediterranean-style eating pattern may be many: improved weight loss, better control of blood glucose (sugar) levels and reduced risk of depression, to name a few.

THE HEART OF IT

The Mediterranean diet is focused on food and lifestyle choices that have significant coronary benefits, including helping prevent heart disease and keeping cholesterol levels in check.

BY HALLIE LEVINE

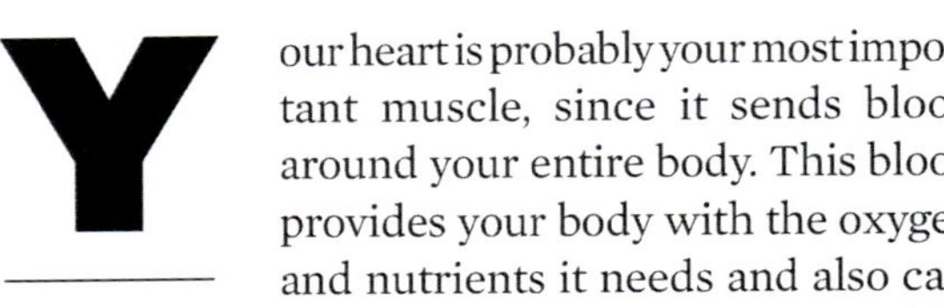

Your heart is probably your most important muscle, since it sends blood around your entire body. This blood provides your body with the oxygen and nutrients it needs and also carries away carbon dioxide and other waste materials.

Yet so few of us take care of it the way we should. Heart disease is the leading cause of death for American adults in the United States, with one person dying every 36 seconds in this country from cardiovascular disease, according to the Centers for Disease Control and Prevention. But at least 200,000 deaths each year from heart disease and stroke are preventable, according to the CDC, with research suggesting that about half of all deaths could be prevented through diet alone.

Enter the Mediterranean diet. This cuisine, based on the eating patterns of folks who live in countries that surround the Mediterranean Sea, such as Greece and Italy, focuses on plant-based foods and plenty of heart-healthy fats. Its historical roots trace back to the Middle Ages. "It's not a diet so much as a way of eating that focuses on whole, unprocessed foods," explains Donald Lloyd-Jones, M.D., chair of the department of preventive medicine at Northwestern University's Feinberg School of Medicine in Chicago and a spokesperson for the American Heart Association. Best of all, it's easy to stick to and absolutely delicious.

The Mediterranean diet is an eating pattern that's been around in some form for thousands of years, based on the dietary habits of the people of Crete. But it became the subject of intensive research about a half century ago, when Ancel Keys, Ph.D., a professor from the University of Minnesota, conducted his "Seven Countries Study," which

looked at the health outcomes of nearly 13,000 middle-aged men in the United States, Japan, Italy, Greece, the Netherlands, Finland and what was then Yugoslavia. What Keys and his colleagues found was startling: While Finland had a whopping 171 heart disease deaths per thousand, and the U.S. had 92 per thousand, Crete in Greece, by comparison, had only 3 per thousand. It turned out that in Crete, the postwar "poor man's" diet—rich in homemade minestrone, pasta with tomato sauce, lots of fresh veggies sprinkled with olive oil, fresh fruit for dessert and a very small portion of meat or fish—was protective against heart disease, explains Walter Willett, M.D., Dr.P.H., professor of epidemiology and nutrition at the Harvard T.H. Chan School of Public Health and professor of medicine at Harvard Medical School.

There are a few reasons the Mediterranean diet may pack such a potent punch when it comes to heart health. Chief among them are the healthy fats that are a mainstay of the diet, says Willett. These include olive oil, nuts and seeds, which all contain monounsaturated fat and have been shown to lower total cholesterol and low-density lipoprotein (LDL, or "bad") cholesterol levels, as well as fatty fish, such as mackerel, albacore tuna and salmon, which are chock-full of omega-3 fatty acids, a type of polyunsaturated fat that reduces inflammation in the body and lowers triglycerides. Willett adds that these healthier fats may also replace other

types of saturated fat in a person's diet—for example, dipping bread in olive oil instead of butter, or eating seafood instead of steak. While there's an evolving debate about how unhealthy saturated fats actually are, these types of fats appear to raise the risk of heart disease when eaten in excess. "Like so many things, saturated fats need to be consumed in moderation," stresses Willett.

Also key are the many fruits, vegetables and whole grains found in the Mediterranean diet. "We know that a plant-based diet can help reduce blood pressure and cholesterol and improve your body's sensitivity to insulin," points out Sean Heffron, M.D., a cardiologist and assistant professor of medicine at NYU Langone Health. An April 2019 review published in the journal *Circulation* analyzed 36 studies and found that people who ate plant proteins, such as soy or nuts, in place of red meat saw significant decreases in both their total and LDL cholesterol. "These foods are full of nutrients that have anti-inflammatory properties," explains Heffron. The Mediterranean diet allows red wine in moderation; wine contains polyphenols, such as resveratrol, that may help protect the lining of blood vessels in your heart. But since too much alcohol intake carries other risks, such as cancer and liver and pancreatic disease, it's important to drink moderately, which is defined by the American Heart Association as no more than one drink a day for women and two a day for men under age 65.

It's also thought that antioxidants found in fruits, vegetables, nuts and whole grains—all bountiful in the Mediterranean diet—can help preserve the length of telomeres, which are a specific part of your DNA that naturally shortens with age. The longer they are, the more protective they are against chronic age-related diseases, such as heart disease, notes Lloyd-Jones. A 2014 Harvard study of more than 4,600 healthy middle-aged women published in the *British Medical Journal* found that those who more closely followed the Mediterranean diet had longer telomeres.

Just as important as what you are eating is what you're not eating, adds Willett, and that includes the fact that most people following a Mediterranean diet steer clear of sugar-sweetened beverages and sugary desserts. A high sugar intake is thought to be bad for your ticker because it raises blood pressure, triglycerides, total cholesterol and LDL cholesterol, according to a 2014 review published in the medical journal *Open Heart*. Consuming a lot of sugar also tends to increase weight and inflammation levels in general, which adds to one's overall heart-disease risk.

There are also lifestyle reasons a Mediterranean-based eating pattern may be protective for your heart. "People who pursue this eating pattern tend to be more active," Lloyd-Jones says. "Their style of eating is also very different: it tends to be slower and less rushed, and they take the time to stop and really savor their meal." As a result, people often feel more satisfied with fewer calories.

The Mediterranean diet also keeps weight—another risk factor for heart disease—in check. A 2016 review published in the *American Journal of Medicine* found that people who follow a Mediterranean diet lose between 9 and 22 pounds and still keep it off after a year, even without any other lifestyle changes. Another 2016 study, published in the medical journal *The Lancet*, followed people between the ages of 55 and 80 for seven years and showed that those who followed a non-calorie-restricted Mediterranean-style diet actually slightly lost weight and gained less fat around their middles than a control group. "Simply choosing the foods that are consistent with the Mediterranean food pyramid are bound to be beneficial for your waistline because they provide more filling fiber and calorie-poor fruits and veggies," explains Roxana Ehsani, M.S., R.D., a Las Vegas nutritionist and spokesperson for the Academy of Nutrition and Dietetics. It's also a high-protein diet, from both animal sources, such as fatty fish, and plant sources, such as legumes, she adds, which is important in helping stave off age-related muscle loss. Since the diet is rich in healthy fats, you'll feel fuller, so you'll be more content to eat less.

While many cardiologists enthusiastically endorse the Mediterranean diet to patients, some also talk up the DASH diet, which stands for Dietary Approaches to Stop Hypertension. It focuses on fruits, vegetables and whole grains, with protein coming from low-fat dairy, fish, poultry and nuts. As in the Mediterranean diet, red meat, sweets and sugary drinks are limited. The main difference between the two is the Mediterranean diet's emphasis on heart-healthy fats, while the DASH diet prioritizes low-fat dairy, says Lloyd-Jones. "There are substantial health benefits to both: They both help with weight loss, lower blood pressure and inflammation and overall reduce cardiovascular risk," he explains. "That's why I tell patients to simply choose the one that makes the most sense to them. The DASH diet often feels more familiar to people because it more closely fits into an American style of eating. That's often why my patients gravitate toward it." If you really don't want to give up your (occasional) serving of red meat and love dairy, DASH may be easier to follow. But if you love feasting on high-fat plant-based fare like hummus, olive oil and nuts, you'll probably have great success with a Mediterranean way of dining.

You should absolutely, however, opt for a Mediterranean diet over the traditional low-fat diet that was often advocated by cardiologists in the 1980s. Many people simply replaced the fat with carbohydrates and as a result ended up gaining weight, notes Willett. "That was when the research on the Mediterranean diet really opened my eyes—here were people who were consuming 45% of their calories from fat but had the longest life expectancy in the world," he says. "It became quickly clear that all fats were not created equal and that low fat was not the way to go." Case in point: The PREDIMED study found that compared with a low-fat diet that kept fat intake under 25 to 30% of total calories, the Mediterranean way of eating reduced risk of major heart disease events like heart attack or stroke by 30%. "Healthy fats like olive oil and nuts don't just fight heart disease—they are satiating, which means you're less likely to overeat," Willett explains. A 2019 Israeli study published in the *Journal of Hepatology* found that people who followed the Mediterranean diet for 18 months had a dramatic reduction in visceral fat (a type of fat that pads the abdomen and internal organs, such as the liver, and has been linked to an increased risk of heart disease) compared with those who followed just a low-fat diet.

Fad diets, such as keto, Whole30 and paleo, may be tempting but should be avoided, Willett stresses. These tend to have high levels of saturated fat, which is bad for heart health, and they also often cut out entire food groups. "If you avoid things like whole grains or even fruit, you're robbing your body of valuable nutrients that are protective against heart disease," he explains.

If you are following the Mediterranean diet, remember that while it's chock-full of good-for-you fats like olive oil and nuts, these foods are still high in calories. "If you deep-fry food in olive oil, you're going to gain weight—that's very different from tossing a tablespoon onto your salad or grilled vegetables," stresses Ehsani. Her recommendation: Limit heart-healthy oils to a couple of tablespoons a day and keep nuts to under 1/4 cup—the equivalent of a handful or less—each day. That way you'll get all their benefits while being mindful of the extra calories.

But when it comes to a healthy diet, it's also important to adopt one that you can stick with. "If you're finding the Mediterranean eating style hard to stick to, then start by incorporating a few small changes, such as adding in an extra serving of fruits or vegetables and eating nuts and fatty fish a couple days a week," suggests Ehsani. Even these small changes in your eating pattern can go a long way toward overall heart health if they are maintained over time.

However, for best results, try to adopt the plan in its entirety. "The most important thing to take away from the Mediterranean way of eating is you want to focus on real food, not something that you take out of a plastic bag or microwave out of a plastic box," says Lloyd-Jones. "As long as you focus on that and enjoy leaner proteins, like chicken or fish, that are cooked in healthy fats, then you can be pretty sure that you're following this eating style. And, really, what could be more natural—or delicious—than some whole-grain bread dipped in olive oil?" *Mangia,* indeed. ●

HEALTHY SNACKS TO HAVE ON HAND INCLUDE HUMMUS, SALSA AND VEGETABLES FOR DIPPING.

ALL ABOUT OLIVE OIL

Here we dish on everything about this Mediterranean-diet staple, from its health benefits to how to store it, plus our secrets on which olive oil is best and how to use it.

JESSICA BALL, M.S., R.D.

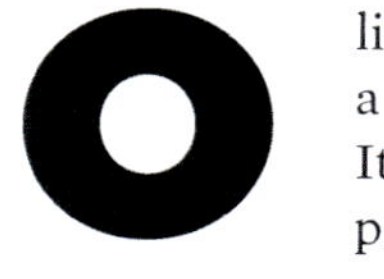

Olive oil gets a lot of credit for being a healthy fat, and for good reason. It has many health benefits, from protecting against heart disease to potentially warding off cancer cell growth. Plus, it's a versatile oil to use in the kitchen, which is why you'll find it in so many of our healthy recipes. Here we'll answer all your questions about the oil—like "What should I use olive oil for?" "Does olive oil go bad?" and even "Can dogs have olive oil?"—so you can see which olive oil is best for you. Spoiler: Olive oil is OK for dogs to eat, if you feel inclined to split your bruschetta with your pup.

One tablespoon of olive oil contains 120 calories, 0 grams carbohydrates, 0 grams protein and 14 grams fat, which includes 2 grams saturated fat, 10 grams monounsaturated fat and 1 gram polyunsaturated fat.

The mono- and polyunsaturated fats are the heart-healthy kind that help keep cholesterol levels in a healthy range, which helps ward off heart disease and other chronic diseases. Saturated fats typically come from animal sources, but there are small amounts found naturally in plant-based oils. While it's important not to eat too much saturated fat, keeping it to under 5 to 6% of your daily calories, as recommended by the American Heart Association, means it's OK to have up to 13 grams per day (on a 2,000-calorie diet).

A study published in the journal *Lipids* analyzed the effect of oleic acid, a main component of olive oil, on inflammation. Researchers found that as consumption of monounsaturated fats like olive oil went up, inflammation levels went down. The type of inflammation they studied is commonly seen as a precursor to heart disease and chronic conditions.

The anti-inflammatory effects of oleuropein, a component found in olive oil, might also protect against diabetes and promote weight loss, as reported by a study in the journal *Biochemistry*.

A newly identified compound called elenolide could be behind olive oil's heart-healthy properties. A study published in the *Journal of the Science of Food and Agriculture* found elenolide in the majority of more than 2,000 olive oils sampled. Elenolide is characterized as an anti-hypertensive agent, which is a fancy way of saying it helps prevent high blood pressure. The higher the quality of the olive oil, the more elenolide is present. In another study, olive oil consumption was linked to up to a 17% reduced risk of cardiovascular disease and stroke compared with the consumption of other types of oils, giving you all the more reason to get your fill of this healthy fat.

Extra-virgin has more polyphenols and fewer free fatty acids than virgin olive oil, but both are equally healthy and nutritious options.

A recent study analyzed the diets of adults from Greece and several Mediterranean islands to see how olive oil related to aging. The authors found that those who used olive oil exclusively as their dietary fat had significant improvements in the successful aging index, which is a measure of age-related lifestyle, social and clinical factors. These findings were especially strong for people over 70 years old. A study published in the *Annals of Clinical and Translational Neurology* had similar findings regarding the brain-protective effects of olive oil. The researchers concluded that a diet rich in extra-virgin olive oil may improve symptoms of Alzheimer's disease by improving the body's ability to clear out dead or damaged cells.

Phytochemicals in olive oil may also block the formation of tumors by suppressing drug-resistant malignant cells, particularly in breast cancers, according to a recent study. Research published in the journal *Nutrients* found that oleacein, another component in olive oil, can reduce the growth of many cancers. These exciting advancements in cancer research are ones to watch, especially when they point to food as medicine.

HERE IS A LITTLE MORE ON WHAT OLIVE OIL labels actually mean: Extra-virgin and virgin oils are processed by being pressed without heat to extract oil from olive plants. The main difference between the two is that extra-virgin olive oil must be pressed within 24 hours after the olives are picked. Nutritionally, the two are similar: extra-virgin has more polyphenols and fewer free fatty acids than virgin olive oil, but both are equally healthy and nutritious options.

Additionally, oils can be filtered or unfiltered, meaning they still contain parts of the olive flesh. The major difference here is that unfiltered oils have a shorter shelf life.

"Light" or "extra light" are marketing terms, typically used to indicate highly refined oils. These terms refer to a milder flavor but have no definition and are no reflection of calorie or fat content.

Olive oil has a shorter shelf life than many people realize, only about 18 to 24 months once bottled. This is because exposure to light and oxygen can make olive oils turn rancid and lose their flavor (and their polyphenol content). Buy olive oil in opaque containers and store it out of direct light to make it last. If you don't regularly use this type of oil, try buying small containers to prevent waste.

There is a lot of controversy on when to use olive oil and how to cook with it. This mainly stems from debate about olive oil's smoke point, which is the temperature at which the oil literally starts to smoke (and may catch fire if it continues to be heated). Heating to this point starts to degrade the oil and breaks down its health-promoting compounds. Olive oil has a smoke point between 365° and 420°F. It is a great oil to enjoy raw in salad dressings or to sauté vegetables up to medium heat. If you are frying or using another very-high-heat cooking method, consider subbing it out for another oil, such as canola oil.

The short answer to the question "Is olive oil healthy?" is yes. It's a great product with nutritional benefits and anti-inflammatory and anti-carcinogenic potential. And when you know how to choose, store and use your olive oil for the best results (for your health and your plate), you'll get the most out of it. Now that you've got the details, let's get cooking! ●

OLIVE THE GOOD STUFF

Turns out this Mediterranean diet staple has health and beauty benefits.

BY CHRISTINA VERCELLETTO

AS PLUMP AND ENTICING as it looks, an olive plucked and eaten right off the tree is appallingly bitter. But the flesh is rich in healthy oils, which may explain why we bothered with the fruit after that first astringent bite.

Indeed, people in the eastern Mediterranean region—where olives are a cultural icon—have been reaping their oil for 6,000 years. In Greece, it's traditional to plant an olive tree when a baby is born. Early Olympic torches burned bright on olive oil. And olive oil is a cornerstone of the much-ballyhooed Mediterranean diet.

Decades of research has borne out notable health perks of olive oil. Its main fatty acid—a monounsaturated fat called oleic acid—and the polyphenols it contains have been shown to reduce inflammation and lower heart disease risk and may have cancer-fighting properties. (Extracts from olive leaves have been shown to have similar effects and are sold as supplements.)

And can we talk beauty benefits? Used straight out of the bottle, olive oil can pull duty as a makeup remover, a shine-imparting hair smoother and a skin moisturizer. Not ready to slather oil directly on your skin? Olive oil can be found in many skin-care products, namely serums and facial oils. You can also rub ¼ cup of olive oil into your hair and let it sit in a shower cap for 15 minutes for a DIY hair mask.

TAKE A BITE OUT OF THE BLUES

As if reducing your risk of heart disease, cancer and type 2 diabetes weren't enough, the Mediterranean diet also works wonders on your mood.

BY HOLLY PEVZNER

Want a quick mood tweak? Down a coffee for an energy boost, enjoy some ice cream or french fries for a little bump in joy, or sit down with a big bowl of chicken soup to feel comfort. "We all seem to understand that these types of foods can offer a temporary mood change," says Elizabeth Somer, R.D., author of *Food & Mood*. But here's the thing: Rocky road won't lead you down a path to more energy and less anxiety. That side of fries won't buoy your brain health and ward off depression. And while chicken soup may very well soothe the soul, having a daily serving between a skipped breakfast and a salty, fatty dinner will do absolutely nothing positive for your state of mind. What just might? Following the research-backed, mood-enhancing Mediterranean-style diet, brimming with produce, whole grains, nuts and other healthy bites.

A groundbreaking 2017 report in *BMC Medicine* found that following this type of diet significantly reduced depression symptoms when compared with the standard American diet (SAD for short, natch), which is jam-packed with processed foods and refined carbohydrates and sorely lacking in produce, beans, nuts and fish. Another study, a 2019 randomized controlled trial in the journal *PLOS One*, found that adults who followed this eating pattern reported lower levels of anxiety and stress along with a significant decrease in depression symptoms after just three weeks. "Most depression treatments require three to four weeks to work, and this was no exception," says study co-author Dick Stevenson, Ph.D. "While simply believing that eating healthy is good for your mind and can propel improvement, with the Mediterranean diet, we know that various

components actually affect brain neurochemistry in a positive way."

Of course, shoehorning one or two Greek salads into your otherwise not-too-healthy weekly mix isn't going to do much for your mood. Instead, the Mediterranean diet aids your brain when you consistently build meals around plant-based foods and other Mediterranean diet tenets. It works when whole grains elbow out processed foods, you choose fish more often than red meat, and you dial back the dairy, poultry and eggs ever so slightly. And as you slowly add more and more Mediterranean-inspired eats and habits into your life, "you'll see improvements in energy, sleep, concentration and mood," says Laura LaChance, M.D., a nutritional psychiatry researcher at McGill University in Montreal. Also mood boosting? Not dieting. "Trading the cycle of restriction and weight gain of traditional dieting for the Mediterranean lifestyle with all it has to choose from has led many of my clients closer to a feeling of sustained happiness," says Supatra Tovar, Psy.D., R.D., a clinical psychologist in Pasadena, California.

A Mediterranean-style diet includes at least 6 to 7 servings of fruit and vegetables each day. That's fresh, baked, roasted, poached, grilled or dried and in all meals and snacks, including dessert. This seems like basic, stay-healthy advice. And it is. But it's also stellar keep-your-brain-healthy advice. "Fruits and vegetables are rich in anti-inflammatory and antioxidant components that directly protect the brain from inflammation," says Camille Lassale, Ph.D., an epidemiologist at Hospital del Mar Research Institute in Barcelona, Spain, who studies how nutrition impacts mental health. That's important because inflammation is connected to various mental health conditions, including cognitive decline, depression and other mood disorders, notes a 2020 report in the *British Medical Journal.*

Somer urges folks to go for deeply colored produce, which is packed with the most antioxidant-rich vitamins and phytonutrients. That's the stuff that will garner the best brain rewards. "Dark green vegetables, in particular, are some of the most mood- and energy-enhancing foods on the planet," she says. In fact, spinach, romaine, kale, broccoli and Brussels sprouts are all considered top antidepressant foods, according to Dr. LaChance's 2018 report in the *World Journal of Psychiatry*. Also on the list: berries and citrus fruits, which are full of vitamin C. "Vitamin C helps curb the stress response by lowering hormone levels and possibly reducing blood pressure," says Somer. "People even report that they feel calmer when they consume enough vitamin C." Plus, C helps the body absorb iron and maintain healthy red blood cells that carry oxygen to every cell in the body, including those of the brain. To get into the Mediterranean vibe, try folding your veggies into sauces, stews and pasta dishes and dress them in olive oil. On the fruit front, add dried fruit to a snack board, a bowl of oatmeal or any salad.

Remember that 2019 report that found those who follow a Mediterranean diet had lower levels of anxiety, stress and depressive symptoms after three weeks? An integral part of the eating plan in the study included increasing consumption of whole grains to three servings a day. Part of the reason is that grains like whole wheat, whole oats, brown rice, rye, barley, buckwheat and more are fiber-rich carbohydrates. "Carbohydrates are the main source of energy for the brain and body," explains Julia Cassidy, R.D.N., the chair-elect of behavioral health nutrition through the Academy of Nutrition and Dietetics. "We need carbs for the brain to properly function; for blood sugar to remain stable; and for neurotransmitters, or brain chemicals, to remain healthy." However, eating refined carbs that don't contain a balance of fiber—like white bread, white rice and packaged foods made with white flour—offers only a flash of energy followed by a mood crash. "You'll wind up with unstable blood sugar that can lead to feelings of frustration and anxiety and food cravings," says Cassidy. "It's always a better idea to eat carbohydrates that are high in fiber and nutrient-rich, which allows blood sugar levels to be better maintained, resulting in a slower release of energy with no crash." Both high-fiber diets and Mediterranean diets promote a diverse gut microbiome, which is associated with a reduced likelihood of depression, according to a 2016 report from the Gerontological Society of America.

A major tenet of the Mediterranean diet is that plants take center stage. And that spotlight extends beyond fruits and vegetables to shine on nuts and legumes too. Indeed, the diet recommends 2 to 4 servings of nuts and legumes each and every day, including things like cannellini and black beans, chickpeas, lentils, peas, walnuts, almonds and more. (One serving of legumes is about ½ cup cooked beans or peas. As for nuts, you're looking at 7 to 8 walnuts or pecans; 20 peanuts; or 12 to 15 almonds per serving.) "That kind of healthy nut and legume consumption is linked to positive mental and cognitive health," says Tovar. That's because both are chock-full of brain-boosting anti-inflammatory and antioxidant components like those in fruits and vegetables.

People in the cities and towns that line the Mediterranean Sea, of course, make fish-based meals a part of their every day. Not only is the seafood fresh and abundant, but regularly eating it is great for health and mood. In fact, Mediterranean faves like oysters, clams, mussels, tuna and salmon are among the best antidepressant foods, according to the 2018 study. Seafood and fish contain copious amounts of vitamin B_{12}, which plays a role in producing neurotransmitters that affect mood and other brain functions; zinc, which helps modulate the brain's response to stress; and the famed omega-3 fatty acids. "Omega-3s, especially docosahexaenoic acid, or DHA, help bolster mood, sharpen the mind, reduce inflammation and improve blood supply to the brain, which works to lower your chance of getting depression and dementia," says Somer, who ranks salmon as her fave. "Include at least two 4-ounce servings weekly, and choose wild salmon when it is affordable, since it is higher in omega-3s." (Other oily fish, such as mackerel, herring, sardines and farmed trout, are high in DHA too.)

The Mediterranean-style diet is not all about diet. In fact, the base of its food pyramid is enjoying meals with friends and family, "and it's extremely impactful to overall mood improvements," says Cassidy. "This feeling of community activates neurotransmitters in the brain that create a sense of belonging and connectedness." In addition, frequent family meals are strongly associated with positive moods and fewer depressive symptoms, according to a 2013 report on adolescents in the *Journal of Paediatrics and Child Health.* It's also a good bet that distractions like TVs and phones are more apt to be out of the picture when dining with others. "This really allows you to fully immerse yourself into treasuring every bite and to laugh and talk while eating," says Tovar. "When you're engaged in the present moment like this, you're not ruminating on the past or worrying about the future. Instead, you're in that sweet spot where I believe peace, joy and calm reside." ●

EAT FOR BRAIN HEALTH

What you eat and what you don't may have a huge impact on your mind. Scientists are discovering that the MIND diet, which is rooted in Mediterranean principles, can help you stay as sharp as a tack.

BY MELINDA WENNER MOYER

Susan Avery seemed more at home in the supermarket than a box of cereal. Wielding a coffee in one hand and a menu she had printed at home in the other, she rolled her shopping cart over to the bakery, hunting for the perfect whole-grain loaf. She spotted a man wearing a black Wegmans cap and solicited his help. "Sir? Can you tell me—Chet? Do you have any other than just this one whole-wheat?"

Avery was being picky because she's on a diet. Not a diet to lose weight, but a diet to nourish her brain. As a professor in her 60s at Ithaca College in New York, Avery is especially keen to keep her mind sharp, yet recently she has had trouble remembering words. In the grocery store a few moments later, I watched as she fumbled to recall that the large packages of beans she likes are called family packs. Avery's aunt suffered from Alzheimer's disease, the devastating condition that currently afflicts 5.8 million Americans, robbing them of their memory and cognition. Avery wants to avoid that fate. Right now, Alzheimer's has no cure: Doctors have run more than 500 clinical trials on potential drugs, but none has prevented the disease or significantly slowed its course. And the Centers for Disease Control and Prevention estimates that by 2050, 14 million Americans will suffer from it.

So when Avery came across the *U.S. News & World Report* diet rankings in 2016 and discovered that the No. 2 best overall diet, the MIND diet, was supposed to be especially good for the brain, she decided to give it a shot. "It just made sense to me," says Avery, whose low voice and deadpan delivery remind me a bit of Tyne Daly

from classic TV's *Cagney & Lacey*. She's been following the diet ever since. She invited me to join her that day to introduce me to the diet.

My grandmother had Alzheimer's. She died when I was young, but I recall that my grandfather became her full-time caregiver. By the end, Alzheimer's patients like my grandmother lose not only their memory but also their ability to care for themselves. So there I was with Avery—watching her pile multigrain bread, wild-caught salmon, spinach, broccoli, squash and mushrooms into her shopping cart. My mission: to understand more about how the MIND diet feeds her brain.

Some might call Avery crazy for thinking that a diet could stave off Alzheimer's. A large part of the medical community scoffs at the idea that something as simple as diet could fend off this debilitating disease. But a growing body of research stands in the face of popular opinion. Much of this research comes from the lab of the late Martha Clare Morris, Sc.D., a nutritional epidemiologist at Rush University Medical Center in Chicago. She spent decades researching how food influences cognition and used her discoveries to create the MIND diet. MIND stands for Mediterranean-DASH Intervention for Neurodegenerative Delay. It is based on the Mediterranean diet and the DASH diet (Dietary Approaches to Stop Hypertension), but it focuses on foods that have been specifically shown to boost brain health. Morris found that people who eat more of certain foods—red meat, sweets, saturated fats—are more likely to develop Alzheimer's, while people who load up on berries, fish, whole grains, nuts, beans, olive oil and, perhaps most important, leafy green vegetables, such as spinach, kale and broccoli, tend to stay healthy. In two studies published in 2015, Morris and her colleagues reported that older adults (participants were in their 70s and 80s) who closely followed this eating pattern were less likely to develop Alzheimer's, plus they scored better on cognitive tests than those who hadn't.

Yet Morris said the MIND diet is not just for older people. Alzheimer's can take decades to develop; a 2013 study reported that the signature amyloid plaques begin to accumulate in the brain 20 years—two decades—before symptoms start. Even people who are not destined to get Alzheimer's are still at risk for age-related cognitive decline, which can start to take root as early as age 30. We don't always know where our brains are headed, but what we eat throughout our lives may shape their final destination.

Food for Thought

Morris had investigated the idea of a brain-focused diet for decades. After she earned her doctorate in epidemiology at the Harvard School of Public Health and ran an important aging study in Iowa, Rush University Medical Center in Morris's hometown, Chicago, recruited her to lead a study teasing out the various lifestyle factors—including foods—that might protect against Alzheimer's disease. "At the time, there was no nutrition research on neurodegenerative diseases like Alzheimer's, so I thought I had to study it," says Morris.

This was a monster of a study. "We sent a team of census takers to every house and apartment in three South Side Chicago communities," she explained to me one especially cold, snowy morning over a coffee (no cream or sugar) in 2018. They ended up following nearly 4,000 healthy older adults for 20 years, interviewing them every three years to understand their lifestyle habits and giving some of them neurological tests. In another study that she started in 1997, which is still ongoing, Morris's colleagues are tracking the lifestyle habits of nearly 1,000 adults in retirement homes and senior public housing complexes while also giving them regular neurological tests. These large epidemiological studies are among the best ways to gain insight into which dietary habits might influence health.

Over time, analyzing their own findings and those of other researchers, Morris and her colleagues teased out which foods seemed brain-healthy and which were not. They then created a list of 15 (10 "good" foods and 5 "bad") and analyzed the eating habits of their study participants with a focus on these foods. Eating good foods earned participants MIND points, and eating bad foods detracted from their scores. Then, in a litmus test, they compared the diet scores with how well each participant did on neurological tests over time. The results were inspiring: People with the highest MIND scores were indeed less likely to develop Alzheimer's disease (53% less likely, in fact) than people with the lowest diet scores. And on cognitive tests, they performed as if they were 7½ years younger.

Building the Case

Still, it's one thing to say that the brain requires certain nutrients and quite another to claim that nutrition can prevent a disease like Alzheimer's. After all, Alzheimer's has a strong genetic component: genetic mutations can directly incite early-onset cases that afflict people under 60. But what many might not know is that most of the time, a blend of genetic and lifestyle factors causes Alzheimer's. When Morris gave genetic tests to the individuals in her studies, she found that among those who had gene mutations known to increase Alzheimer's risk, the MIND diet was less protective, but it still made a difference.

And if you consider what happens to the brain when the disease takes hold, the ties to nutrition become clearer. Over time, the brain gets severely damaged by inflammation as well as by oxidative stress. These processes disrupt cell function and lead to the buildup of plaques and tangles. Once the cells become very injured, they die, and as the cell death spreads, Alzheimer's sets in.

The thing about inflammation and oxidative stress is that certain nutrients can potentially mitigate them, both in the brain and in the rest of the body. And some others, such as saturated fat and sugar, can ramp up the body's production of compounds that incite inflammation. To better understand the connection between genes and lifestyle, I spoke with Trish Whitaker, a former schoolteacher living in Conway, Arkansas, who is in her late 60s. "I'm from the South—from the land where they roll it in sugar and butter and then fry it," she explained to me in a soft Arkansas accent. Whitaker knows how strong the genetic connection to Alzheimer's can be. Both of her parents, as well as both of her sisters, developed the disease. But an October 2015 meeting with Richard Isaacson, M.D.—a neurologist who directs the Alzheimer's Prevention Clinic at Weill Cornell Medicine and New York–Presbyterian in Manhattan—inspired Whitaker to become much more careful about what she ate. It was Whitaker's daughter who discovered Dr. Isaacson. She had come across his book, *The Alzheimer's Diet*—which has recommendations similar to

RICH IN ANTIOXIDANTS, STRAWBERRIES AND OTHER BERRIES SHOULD BE EATEN TWICE A WEEK.

those Morris proposes for the types of foods that could stave off Alzheimer's—and encouraged her mom to read it. Whitaker was so intrigued that she drove 1,300 miles to see Isaacson in person.

Oxidative stress is the other damaging process associated with Alzheimer's that can build up throughout the body and wreak havoc. All day our cells use nutrients to make energy, releasing tiny, powerful molecules (free radicals) as waste, causing damage to cells. But free radicals are neutralized by molecules called antioxidants. Foods like leafy greens and berries happen to be very rich in antioxidants, so when we eat them, we provide our bodies with greater means to reduce oxidative stress. One class of antioxidants called flavonoids, found in blueberries and strawberries, has been shown in animal studies to protect vulnerable neurons and help neurons regenerate. The antioxidant vitamin E (good sources include almonds, spinach and sunflower seeds) sits on the outer layer of brain cells "to snatch up free-radical molecules right when they occur so that they can't harm the cell," Morris says.

There's an interesting story to tell about sugar when it comes to the brain too. In the 1980s, researchers discovered that insulin, the hormone made by the pancreas that regulates blood sugar levels, can cross the blood-brain barrier. Although brain insulin doesn't have the same sugar-controlling job, it plays a role in learning and memory. These findings piqued the interest of Suzanne de la Monte, M.D., a neurosurgeon and pathologist at Brown University, who decided in 2005 to compare brain insulin levels in healthy people and those with Alzheimer's. She found that brain processes involving insulin are severely impaired in Alzheimer's, which led her to start calling Alzheimer's "type 3 diabetes." This implicates diets because a sugar-rich diet interferes with insulin signaling and sensitivity throughout the body. In fact, people with type 2 diabetes, a disease characterized by reduced insulin sensitivity, are more than twice as likely to develop Alzheimer's.

Playing Defense

Morris, Isaacson and de la Monte's work isn't the only research to have linked diet to brain health. Several studies have reported that the Mediterranean diet is associated with a lower risk of dementia too. In a study published in January 2017, researchers in the U.K. and Canada reported that people in their 70s who followed a Mediterranean-style diet lost less brain volume over a three-year period than people who did not. In a 2013 study, Spanish researchers put 522 middle-aged-to-older adults on either a Mediterranean diet or a low-fat diet for 6½ years. Subjects following the Mediterranean diet fared much better on cognitive tests at the end of the trial. And a review of 12 studies published in 2013 concluded that greater adherence to the Mediterranean diet was associated with slower cognitive decline and a lower risk of developing Alzheimer's disease.

You might think that the Alzheimer's and

neurology scientific communities would be thrilled by this new bounty of research—finally, a potential way to reduce the toll of Alzheimer's. Mostly, though, they're still doubtful. "I get made fun of," Isaacson says. "One colleague called me the 'blueberry neurologist.'" Morris told a similar story: "The field of neurology is very skeptical that diet might influence diseases of the brain." When I reached out to the moderator of an Alzheimer's support group on Facebook, whose members include Alzheimer's patients and caregivers, hoping to post a question about diet, I was told not to bother: "Most members don't believe that diet will help."

Why is this idea so controversial? One problem is that many neurologists aren't trained in nutrition, so they don't consider it as potentially important in the development of brain diseases. "I got maybe four hours' worth of nutrition education in my neurology training," Isaacson says, which frustrated him so much he took the initiative to take additional nutrition coursework. And even when neurologists have heard that nutrition could play a role in dementia, they don't always know how much research has now accumulated to support the idea. When Isaacson gets pushback from doctors who scoff at the idea, he replies with: "Guess what? There is evidence, and let's talk about it."

A Mindful Meal

When we arrived back at Susan Avery's house after grocery shopping, she took a bottle of chardonnay from the fridge. "It's 5 o'clock somewhere," she announced. (Where we were, it was 4:30.) The MIND diet recommends one glass of wine a day. Her husband, Doug, who follows MIND with her, was joining us for dinner. He admitted that he'd stopped for fast food on the way home from a lunchtime doctor's appointment. The good news, though, is that even just partially following the diet may have cognitive benefits. Morris's study found that people whose MIND diet scores were in the middle range—6.5 to 8.5 points out of a maximum of 15—were still 35% less likely to develop Alzheimer's compared with people who had the lowest MIND diet scores.

Over our wine, Avery and I talked about how her life has changed on the MIND diet. She used to choose meals primarily on taste and convenience; pasta and red meat were staples. The MIND diet is more work for her in terms of meal planning and shopping—she has a Post-it note stuck to her car's glove compartment to remind her what to eat and what to avoid. We may not yet know exactly how protective the MIND diet is, but with my family history of Alzheimer's and the harsh reality of no cure, I decided then and there that I, too, was going to make some changes—more berries and fish, less sugar and refined carbs.

One thing Morris said to me in Chicago stuck: "The longer you have healthy lifestyle practices, the more long-term benefit you have." Over a dessert of baked pears, I asked Avery whether she had noticed any cognitive changes since starting the diet four months earlier. "Maybe I am forgetting less now, but I think that's almost too simplistic," she said. She can't be sure if the food is truly making a difference or if her expectations are muddying her perspective.

Several studies have reported that the Mediterranean diet is associated with a lower risk of dementia.

Whitaker, who had made her dietary changes more than a year before, was more confident. She said she hadn't had as many forgetful moments as she used to. "Before I went to Dr. Isaacson, anytime I would forget anything, I would say, 'Is Alzheimer's here? Is this the beginning?' I rarely ever say that anymore," she said. "If nothing else, making these changes has reduced my fear quite a bit. Maybe it's because it's given me a measure of control over my life. I am doing something. Every day, I'm doing things to keep my brain healthy." ●

Excerpted from EatingWell: Feel-Good Food: A Happy Path to Better Living *(published in 2019), available on Amazon.*

STAVE OFF INFLAMMATION

Fans of anti-inflammatory diets say these regimens can transform you inside and out. But this Hollywood health "fad" is rooted in the same key principles that make the Mediterranean diet so healthy.

BY SUNNY SEA GOLD

Tom Brady, Venus Williams, Penélope Cruz and Rosie Huntington-Whiteley have something in common, aside from being unnaturally beautiful: They've all followed forms of anti-inflammatory (AI) diets at one time or another. Brady has done it to boost his performance on the football field. Williams said she did it to help keep her autoimmune disorder in check. And Cruz and Huntington-Whiteley have followed an AI-style detox to keep their skin radiant.

These celeb diets may be buzzy, but the tenets of an AI diet—more plants, less sugar, no refined stuff—are the same tentpoles as the Mediterranean diet's. "Who needs to eat a more anti-inflammatory diet? Everyone," says Barry Sears, Ph.D., creator of the Zone diet, who has spent decades studying chronic inflammation.

Believe it or not, inflammation starts as a good thing. It happens when your immune system sends white blood cells and "warrior" compounds like eicosanoids to attack invading viruses, bacteria and toxins. A classic example of totally normal inflammation: pain, heat, redness and swelling around a wound or an injury (think of a tender sprained ankle).

"There's a separate response called resolution that brings the dogs of war back to their barracks and heals your tissues," says Sears. "The first phase of inflammation causes cellular destruction, and the second phase, resolution, begins cellular rejuvenation. As long as those phases are balanced, you stay well."

But for more and more of us, the balance never happens. That's because sugar, refined grains and saturated fat can also trigger an inflammatory immune response, notes Sears, and the typical Western diet is packed with them, meaning we're inflaming our bodies over and over, every time we eat. Meanwhile, guess what the average American gets way too little of: fruits and nonstarchy veggies, which are packed with antioxidants that help cool things down and reduce the intensity of the initial inflammatory response, and fatty fish, a great source of omega-3 fatty acids, which can help move your body into the resolution phase.

Air pollution and environmental toxins also trigger your immune system this way, but "most of the chronic, extra inflammation in our bodies is diet-related," says Sears. In arteries, chronic inflammation can lead to heart disease. In the brain, it's linked to anxiety and depression. In your joints, it causes swelling and pain. In the gut, inflammation throws off the balance of helpful bacteria and causes direct damage to the lining of the intestines, says Mark Hyman, M.D., director of the Center for Functional Medicine at the Cleveland Clinic and author of *The Blood Sugar Solution: 10-Day Detox Diet*. That may contribute to irritable bowel syndrome (IBS), food sensitivities, autoimmune diseases and even obesity, research suggests.

Following a Mediterranean diet is linked to many health benefits, from keeping weight down to slashing the risk for stroke and heart disease.

In contrast, research shows that following a more anti-inflammatory style of eating may reduce the risk of heart disease, obesity and some cancers and may even extend your life, says Frank Hu, M.D., professor of nutrition and epidemiology at the Harvard T.H. Chan School of Public Health. Other claims about anti-inflammatory diets—for example, that they can reverse autoimmune disease (the goal of the Autoimmune Protocol, an extremely restrictive AI diet) or improve mental health—have less solid proof, he says.

There isn't one specific AI diet, unlike Atkins or South Beach. Sears's Zone diet and Dr. Hyman's Detox are both highly anti-inflammatory, as is the soy-heavy plan that integrative medicine guru Andrew Weil, M.D., offers for free on his website. Paleo and Whole30 diets are both AI too.

But the plan with the most research-backed anti-inflammatory cred is the traditional Mediterranean diet, emphasizing fruits, vegetables, whole grains, legumes, fish and olive oil. Several very large studies—including the famed Nurses' Health Study—have found that people who follow a Mediterranean pattern of eating have lower levels of the inflammatory markers C-reactive protein and interleukin-6 in their blood compared with those who don't. This may be one reason the Mediterranean diet is linked to so many health benefits, from keeping weight down to slashing heart and stroke risk, notes Dr. Hu.

The goals of an AI plan are simple: Cut way back on foods that trigger an inflammatory response and eat more of the foods that heal damage. While there are some variations on what's allowed and what isn't, most AI plans share an emphasis on eating whole, minimally processed foods, nonstarchy vegetables, monounsaturated fats like olive oil and avocado, colorful berries and other fruit, and lots of omega-3s from fatty fish (or supplements), and avoiding added sugar and refined grains.

You don't have to follow any AI diet perfectly to make a big impact, say our experts. A healthy body is built to handle the occasional onslaught of inflammation (like having a cupcake at a party); it's the regular, consistent consumption (and over-consumption) of inflammatory foods like sugar and saturated fat that's linked to serious disease, says Sonya Angelone, R.D.N., a spokesperson for the Academy of Nutrition and Dietetics.

A 2012 study of nearly 2,000 people, for example, found that those who ate the most sweets over two years had significantly higher levels of interleukin-6 than people who ate more veggies, fruits and whole grains.

That's why it's more important to eat an overall "super" diet rather than focus on individual superfoods, says Angelone. "If you're regularly eating a bunch of doughnuts along with a bunch of anti-inflammatory veggies, you're still harming your body," adds Dr. Hyman. Follow these guidelines on most days:

1. Aim for half to two-thirds of your plate to be nonstarchy vegetables (think greens of all kinds, mushrooms, summer squash, beets, cauliflower . . . the

DARK LEAFY GREENS PACK NUTRIENTS, MOST NOTABLY LUTEIN, FOLATE AND VITAMIN K, THAT SLOW THE SIMMER OF INFLAMMATION.

list goes on and on)—ideally at breakfast, too, says Dr. Hyman. They're packed with gut-balancing fiber and powerful antioxidants.

2. Limit added sugar and sweet drinks. That includes fruit juices and natural sweeteners like honey, says Dr. Hyman. In a small 2005 study, people who were fed a high-sugar diet for 10 weeks had significantly elevated blood levels of haptoglobin—an inflammatory marker that in high concentrations is associated with diabetes, heart attack, stroke and obesity—compared with controls.

3. Eat fish, especially fatty kinds like salmon, mackerel, herring and anchovies. (Or take omega-3 supplements—at least 1,000 milligrams daily, says Dr. Hyman.)

4. Nix white flour and limit other flour-based foods. Focus on whole, intact grains like quinoa, brown rice and bulgur wheat instead of loading up on whole-grain crackers, breads and tortillas. Even 100% whole-grain flour will cause a spike in blood sugar that exacerbates inflammation, especially for people with insulin resistance, metabolic syndrome (i.e., prediabetes) or diabetes, so use them moderately, says Sears.

5. Choose fats carefully. The most abundant saturated fats in our diet contain the same fatty acids as do fragments of the cell walls of many bacteria—no wonder your immune system sees a bacon cheeseburger as a threat! Limit saturated fats like butter and skip vegetable oils that are high in omega-6 fats, such as safflower and corn oils. Go for olive, avocado or walnut oil instead.

"It might sound tough, but if you think about it, it's exactly how your grandmother probably told you to eat!" says Sears. A diet endorsed by supermodels and your nana? Now that sounds like a plan.

A SIMPLE AND CUSTOMIZABLE WAY TO MANAGE WEIGHT

One of the best things about the Mediterranean diet is how easy it is to adapt and stick to. That means that the eating plan is not only healthy, it's also a reliable approach for tackling weight-related goals in a nutritious and sustainable way.

BY EMILY JOSHU

For decades, seemingly endless fad diets have popped up to try to solve the ever-present struggle of losing weight. Low-carb, low-fat and low-sodium are just a few of the diets claiming quick-fix weight loss, generally with one thing in common: restriction. Many of the best-known diets of the past, including trendy movements like the ketogenic and paleo diets, prioritize elimination. Since recent research suggests that more than 80% of those who shed significant pounds regained weight after five years, the restrictive nature of these popular diets could be connected to the obstacle of sticking with them.

Within the past decade, however, health professionals have begun looking further back in time, all the way back to the Middle Ages, with the Mediterranean diet. In 2020, *U.S. News and World Report* evaluated 41 of the most renowned diets, ranking the Mediterranean diet as the best overall eating pattern for weight loss. This is because it's bolstered by an array of nutritious foods, including leafy greens, healthy fats, such as those in olive oil, and protein-packed fish, such as salmon, as well as nuts and whole grains. The Mediterranean diet pyramid, an adaptation of the traditional food pyramid, establishes these foods as the core foundation at the bottom, while red meats and sweets sit at the top to be consumed in moderation. While foods with added sugars, refined grains, such as white bread, and red or processed meats are to be eaten sparingly, nothing is excluded entirely from this eating plan. Typically, a Mediterranean eating pattern's star players are single-ingredient, nonprocessed, plant-based finds. "The main parts of a Mediterranean diet,

AS LITTLE AS 30 MINUTES OF PLANNING MEALS WILL MAKE IT EASIER TO STICK TO A WEEK OF MEDITERRANEAN EATING.

what really defines it, is the amount of healthy, plant-based foods that the diet is built on and that it really is an eating plan that any different culture can work with and make it their own," says Liz Weinandy, M.P.H., registered dietitian at the Ohio State University Wexner Medical Center. For a blueprint of Mediterranean-style weight management, Weinandy points to the Department of Health and Human Services and United States Department of Agriculture Dietary Guidelines for Americans, which similarly calls for a diet filled with leafy greens, legumes, fruits, whole grains, dairy, lean meats, eggs and seafood.

While following this eating plan could brighten your plate without the restrictions of other fad diets, its nutrient-rich foods filled with fiber, healthful fats and macronutrients may also be linked to better weight management and even weight loss. A 2016 review of five studies in the *American Journal of Medicine*, for example, found that the Mediterranean diet was as effective as low-carb diets, resulting in up to 22 pounds of weight loss over one year. Additionally, a large 2018 study in the journal *Nutrition & Diabetes* of more than 32,000 people showed that long-term adherence to the Mediterranean diet was associated with a decreased risk of gaining weight and belly fat over a five-year period.

This is because calories and other key nutrients in Mediterranean foods can help you feel fuller longer, also known as food satiety. Weinandy points to the abundant amounts of fiber and healthful fats that stay in the stomach longer. "What the Mediterranean diet does is showcase fiber because of the large amounts of fruits, vegetables, beans and whole grains that are high in fiber, and then also the healthy fats, olive oil, the fat from salmon, nuts and avocados," Weinandy says. Because the food stays in the stomach longer, this leads to delayed gastric emptying, according to Leah Holbrook, M.S., R.D., clinical instructor in the department of family, population and preventative medicine at Stony Brook Medicine. This creates longer-lasting satisfaction, which can lead people to cut down on overeating and excessive snacking. "The comparison would be if someone was eating a fast-food meal," Weinandy says. "It would be highly processed [and] break down very little fiber, and it will break down faster. It raises blood sugars quickly, it will drop them more quickly, and in the end people feel much more hungry and will also eat a lot more because of that lack of fiber." A 2017 study in the *British Journal of Nutrition* found that a nonrestrictive satiating diet, such as the Mediterranean diet, led to twice the decrease in fat-mass percentage compared with a control healthy diet, and participants showed a strong adherence to the plan. Therefore, given the choice between a Big Mac and a turkey burger, the former is more likely to leave you hungry just a couple of hours later at a significantly higher calorie level.

WHILE PACKING YOUR PLATE WITH VITAL NUTRIENTS is a key step in a Mediterranean diet, lacing up your shoes for some light exercise is also essential for managing weight. The Mediterranean diet pyramid even places physical activity directly below its core food groups, so while diet and exercise traditionally complement each other in most diets, the healthfulness of Mediterranean foods particularly boosts the potential for effective weight management. Because a Mediterranean eating pattern spotlights plant-based foods, it can curb calorie intake, which helps you to fuel properly for a run around the block or for a spin class. This is because calories are necessary for staying energized; if you're cutting calories just for the sake of cutting calories, you won't have as much energy to get through the day. These foods are bolstered not only by needed calories, but also by complex carbs, which take longer for the body to digest, leaving you fuller longer. Since other diets may emphasize cutting calories, carbs or fat, you might drop a few pounds, but you'll be left without sustainable amounts of energy.

"Being physically active is obviously very important for weight management. It's also very important for general health, so a Mediterranean diet coupled with activity should hit the mark in terms of appropriate calories in and output through exercise," says Holbrook.

The Mediterranean diet is also highly customizable, so even if you don't like fish or avocados, there's likely an alternative. This also leaves room to experiment in the kitchen with new recipes and cooking methods, decreasing the incentive to order takeout or go to a restaurant that might not have Mediterranean-friendly options. The diet emphasizes cooking at home and eating meals together, which can spark creativity to find something healthful that everyone enjoys. "Cooking food and preparing food at home, although it's time consuming, has to be part of a healthy plan," Holbrook says. Holbrook recommends searching for recipes featuring a Mediterranean diet's key ingredients and finding new ways to incorporate cooking into your schedule, such as through weekly meal planning.

Not only does this customization make the Mediterranean diet easier to stick to, Weinandy says, but it also makes the diet easier to start if you're not used to eating some of its star ingredients. If you've never had whole-grain pasta, for example, try putting half white pasta and half whole-grain pasta into the pot for your next spaghetti night, Weinandy recommends. Since whole-grain pasta takes about 2 to 4 minutes longer to cook, add that to the pot first.

Primarily, Weinandy says, if you're starting a Mediterranean diet for the first time in order to manage your weight, start with small, gradual steps. "Don't think you have to do this 180, because that's where people fail. They think it's either all or nothing." Weinandy says. "We're not trying to completely swing into some other ballpark that we're not familiar with." ●

CHAPTER 2

EXPLORING THE DIET'S ROOTS

The Mediterranean diet offers a cuisine rich in colors, tastes and traditions. Here's a look at some of the places in the Mediterranean from which the eating plan draws its lessons.

THE REAL MEDITERRANEAN DIET

The first detailed study of this storied heart-healthy diet goes all the way back to the 1940s on Crete—the largest of the Greek islands in the Mediterranean. Find out what the island's inhabitants were doing so right. Their lessons might astonish you.

BY PAUL GREENBERG

CRETE, GREECE

In the spring of 1948, an American social scientist named Leland Allbaugh departed for the island of Crete with the intention of fixing it. At the time, Greeks had the lowest per capita income in Europe and Cretans had the lowest income in Greece. Malaria and "diseases of filth," like dysentery, were widespread. All this led Allbaugh to conclude in a letter to his Rockefeller Foundation funders that "the Cretans have a potential need for almost everything." In an attempt to catalog those needs, Allbaugh carried out seven months of intensive field research. Fanning out across the spare, rocky land, he and his team visited farmers' fields and workers' factories, monitored the care of the sick and counted up the ways the moribund had died.

But most important, the Allbaugh group exhaustively inventoried what the Cretans ate. Expecting to find widespread malnutrition, the researchers instead discovered the local diet to be "surprisingly good" and noted that the Cretans had an exceedingly low rate of chronic Western diseases. They suffered about a third as many heart-disease-related deaths as Americans at the time and had barely any incidence of cancer. No matter how underdeveloped Crete might have been in terms of roads, plumbing and other typical markers of "progress," it seemed

AN EVENING VIEW OF AGIOS NIKOLAOS, CRETE, AND ITS HARBOR

they were far ahead of the U.S. when it came to eating well.

And they'd been eating this well for millennia: "The basic foods for the modern Cretan diet are probably the same as during the Minoan period, about 2000 B.C.," Allbaugh wrote in *Crete*, the 572-page book outlining his findings. This diet would be analyzed in an even deeper way a decade later, when University of Minnesota physiologist Ancel Keys, Ph.D., traveled to Crete to interview men from the island's heartland. Once again, subjects were found to be lean and largely free of heart disease and cancer. So healthy were the Cretans that Keys used them as a pilot population for his epic "Seven Countries Study"—the first detailed analysis to compare diet and health outcomes across a broad spectrum of nations. Keys cited Cretans repeatedly as ideal practitioners of a lifestyle that he and his wife, Margaret, termed "the Mediterranean Way."

Ever since, we've been captivated by what has come to be known as the Mediterranean diet. And medical researchers continue to build a huge body of evidence around Allbaugh's and Keys's findings. More than 6,500 scientific papers have been published on the Mediterranean diet, including the 1998 Lyon Diet Heart Study—the first clinical trial on the subject and one that's still cited today. It found a 50 to 70% reduction in rates of heart disease and stroke recurrence among those following a Mediterranean diet.

Then there was the landmark 2013 PREDIMED

study, which observed a 39% reduction in heart attacks in healthy individuals who added key Mediterranean components (namely nuts and olive oil) to their diets. (The paper was retracted and later republished to correct a flaw in the randomization process, but the results remained the same.) Evidence has also linked a Mediterranean style of eating to improved cognition. And a population-level study published in the *New England Journal of Medicine* stated bluntly that "greater adherence to the traditional Mediterranean diet is associated with a significant reduction in total mortality." It is due to this and other research that *U.S. News & World Report* has ranked the diet best in the world for the past three years.

But despite all the acclaim, most Americans remain confused about what a Mediterranean diet really is. Apart from a vague sense of olive oil and red wine being a good idea and a big slab of red meat being a bad one, we often just pick and choose healthy-sounding foods from any one of the countries that the Mediterranean Sea touches without having an organizing principle.

So in an attempt to offer some more concrete advice, I journeyed to Crete to find out exactly what Cretans were eating when Allbaugh and Keys found them in the peak of health. What I learned is that while much of the Cretan tradition can be quixotic and even a little arbitrary, there are specific changes we can make to our American diet that will bring us more in line with the Mediterranean ideal.

Eat Plenty of Carbs—but the Right Carbs

"This really is the base of the original Cretan diet," archaeologist Dimitra Mylona, Ph.D., said as she handed me a tough, thick cracker in the dank chamber of a Minoan tomb a few miles outside the Cretan town of Rethymnon. For the past 20 years, Mylona has been looking at the eating habits of the early inhabitants of the island, through her work with the Institute of Aegean Prehistory Study Center. What she concluded is that it was the rough barley bread, or rusk, that formed the backbone of the diet. "You can see it in their teeth," she told me. "They're worn down and damaged from chewing on this hard stuff." Indeed, Allbaugh found that 39% of Cretans' daily calories came from whole grains.

Whereas wheat was typically eaten by the upper classes or exported, barley was the food of the commoners. This whole grain made for a bread that was slower to digest and less likely to cause the insulin spikes of white flour—thanks largely to barley's high amounts of soluble fiber, nearly twice that of whole wheat. "Fiber has all sorts of benefits in terms of appetite and weight control," explained *EatingWell* adviser David Katz, M.D., M.P.H., director of Yale University's Yale-Griffin Prevention Research Center. Soluble fiber extends the time your body takes to break down carbs and "smooths out" the digestion of sugars and fats, helping you feel fuller longer.

Whole grains high in soluble fiber also have proven heart-health benefits. A recent review of 243 studies published in *The Lancet* found that people who ate the most fiber had a 15% to 30% lower risk of death from heart disease. And the research showed a similar reduction in risk of developing cardiovascular disease, type 2 diabetes and colon cancer. High fiber intake was also linked to lower body weight and lower blood

pressure and cholesterol. All of this resulted in a population that Allbaugh described as "slim-waisted, erect and able to withstand hunger during war and revolutions."

LESSON: While ample carbohydrates were part of the Cretan diet, the vast majority were from whole grains rich in soluble fiber. Meanwhile, just 16% of the grains Americans eat are whole—the rest are refined. Katz said you can follow the Cretan example by switching to 100% whole-wheat bread products and aiming for at least one daily portion of nonwheat grains, like oats or barley. And shoot for around 28 total grams of fiber per day.

Curb Added Sugar

Arguably as important as the type of carbs Cretans ate is the kind they did not. Namely, sugar. Allbaugh recorded a minuscule 50 calories a day from foods like honey and grape must in the local diet—about 3 teaspoons' worth of added sugar. The average American currently gets 23 teaspoons' worth of added sugar daily (more than the Greeks ate in a week). "Cretans do not serve desserts—except for fresh fruit in season," Allbaugh observed. "Cake is seldom served and pie almost never." Even Greek yogurt—one of their culinary claims to fame—was eaten plain.

The healthy components of the different fruits and vegetables Cretans ate was amplified by the sheer quantity they consumed.

Too much sugar in the diet has obvious implications for developing type 2 diabetes, but a 15-year-long study published in *JAMA Internal Medicine* found an association between added sugar and heart disease as well. Those eating a diet high in these refined carbs (about 17% to 21% of daily calories) had a 38% greater risk of dying from heart disease than those who got just 8% of their calories from added sugar. Research Keys and his colleagues conducted decades earlier for the "Seven Countries Study" also revealed an association between sugar intake and cardiovascular disease, albeit a weaker one than for dietary sources of saturated fat.

LESSON: Look for ways to trim added sugars from your diet—including those that may be lurking in your flavored "Mediterranean" Greek yogurt. (Some pack as much per serving as a Twinkie.) The American Heart Association recommends limiting added sugars to 25 grams daily for women and 36 for men, or about 6 and 9 teaspoons' worth. So read labels on packaged items and choose ones with the lowest amount, because those grams can add up quickly.

Expand Your Fruit and Vegetable Repertoire

Under a canopy of 350-year-old olive trees just outside the city of Chaniá, another food- and gastronomy-focused archaeologist, Mariana Kavroulaki, explained that after the Minoan period of self-government ended around 1450 B.C., Cretan food habits were dictated by harsh socioeconomic conditions imposed by the island's later colonizers.

Over the centuries, Crete was conquered and occupied again and again. The island's overlords—Romans, Venetians, Ottomans—all used Crete as a giant plantation, sending the most highly prized agricultural products, such as lemons, figs and raisins, abroad. As a result, Cretans had to eat whatever other foods were left.

But it turns out what was left had great nutritional benefits. Perhaps the greatest example is the wild field greens known as horta that women gathered in the winter and spring months. Spicy and bitter, succulent and sour, horta encompass a broad array of more than 100 edible plants. Some, like purslane, contain high amounts of short-chain omega-3 fatty acids, which have been shown to help reduce blood pressure and cholesterol levels and lower the risk of heart disease and type 2 diabetes. Other greens, like dandelion, have antioxidants that may play a role in warding off cancer.

A wide variety of horta in the diet contributed significantly to the longevity Cretans enjoyed, according to Antonia Trichopoulou, M.D., Ph.D., a prolific Mediterranean diet researcher and president of the nonprofit Hellenic Health Foundation. A study she conducted, published in *BMJ*, found that high consumption of plants

FIND THE RECIPES FOR REVITHIA ME KOLOKYTHA, LEFT, AND HONDROS ME MELITZANES, BELOW, ON PAGES 52 AND 53.

(including greens, as well as onions, tomatoes, cabbage and eggplant) accounted for the largest reduction in early mortality risk compared to the other beneficial aspects of the traditional Mediterranean diet, such as low meat consumption and liberal olive oil intake.

When it came to fruit, Allbaugh noted that the most-consumed items were grapes, pomegranates and melons, all of which score an impressive 118 or higher on the Aggregate Nutrient Density Index (ANDI), a system that rates foods based on their nutrient content. Contrast that with the U.S., where our current top three fruits—apples, oranges and bananas—have ANDI scores of 53, 98 and 30, respectively.

The individual healthy components of the different fruits and vegetables that were eaten by Cretans were amplified by the sheer quantity they consumed—on average, 432 pounds of produce per person annually. Around that time, Americans were eating 323 pounds and today we get around 220. (These totals don't include potatoes, which were—and are—popular with both groups.)

LESSON: The Cretans were models of plant-forward eating long before it was a thing in the U.S. (Author Michael Pollan's oft-quoted maxim to eat "mostly plants" is, by his own admission, derived from the first Crete studies that went on to inspire our modern dietary guidelines.) So: up your produce intake. According to a meta-analysis in *BMJ* that looked at data from nearly 470,000 people, for every daily serving of fruits and vegetables consumed, the risk of dying from heart disease dropped by 4% and the odds of premature death from any cause fell by 5% (with a maximum benefit at about 5 servings a day). And go for variety. Despite the many types of produce available to us today, we often stick to the same ones, and not the most nutritious ones at that.

Michael Greger, M.D., author of *How Not to Die*, suggests rotating as many different colorful fruits and vegetables through your diet as possible to get a broad range of vitamins and minerals. And, generally, the brighter or deeper the pigment—like the dark, leafy horta—the more phytonutrients the food will contain.

TOMATOES ARE NUTRIENT-DENSE, LOW IN CALORIES AND A GREAT SOURCE OF ANTIOXIDANTS.

Enjoy a Little Krasí

Perhaps the greatest point of controversy regarding the Mediterranean diet is the inclusion of red wine (krasí) as an integral component—so much so that it's treated like a nutrient. Over the past 70 years, studies have gone back and forth on the benefits of alcohol (of any kind). Some have found that moderate amounts—about a drink a day for women and two for men—can lower heart disease risk, while others have found no such benefit, or even harm.

What we do know, because Allbaugh recorded it, is that most of the wine Cretans drank was red and they always had it with food. This is important because some research suggests there may be a synergistic effect between wine and food that promotes heart health better than sipping it on its own. Red wine is also rich in

polyphenols—antioxidants including anthocyanins and oleocanthal, the same compound as in olive oil—that have been found to keep platelets from building up and clotting blood vessels and to improve cholesterol and blood vessel function, all of which are cardioprotective. Concentrations of these polyphenols are about 10 times higher in red wine than white (although the latter has beneficial compounds of its own).

Also worth noting: regular wine consumption clearly enhanced a general culture of intergenerational sociability—another key pillar in the health and welfare of long-lived Mediterraneans. But while red wine was had at multiple meals daily, alcohol accounted for only 1% of total calories. (Allbaugh did suspect the Cretans underreported how much they drank because they felt "the visiting Americans might be expected to frown upon heavy wine consumption." By his observations, they had about one small glass a day.)

LESSON: If you don't drink, this is not a reason to start. But if you enjoy the occasional glass of red over a meal with friends and family, it could improve the quality of your life and possibly the length of it.

Choose Good Fat, Not Low Fat

Another dozen miles up the road toward Crete's western shore stands the Olive Tree of Vouves. As big around as a station wagon and estimated at more than 3,000 years old, it is an enduring testament to the fundamental role that olive oil has played in the Cretan diet.

Indeed, Allbaugh noted that "to the foreign visitor, food seemed literally to be 'swimming'

IN THE 1940S, CRETANS ATE TWICE AS MUCH BEANS AND NUTS AS AMERICANS DID AT THE TIME, ACCORDING TO ALLBAUGH. PICTURED: RETHYMNON OLD PORT IN CRETE.

in oil." And when Keys made his observations, he found as much as 40% of daily calories came from it.

Emmanouil Karpadakis, an olive oil tasting expert at Terra Creta olive oil cooperative in Chaniá, told me that 1940s-era Cretans were likely to be consuming olives harvested when still green, and thus richer in antioxidants. As Katz later explained, these greener olives would have contained higher amounts of a compound called oleocanthal, a highly potent antioxidant that gives olive oil its slightly bitter edge.

Oleocanthal has been shown to have anti-inflammatory effects that play a significant role in reducing the risk of chronic diseases, including heart disease, type 2 diabetes and certain kinds of cancer.

According to a study published in the *Journal of Agricultural and Food Chemistry* that compared oleocanthal levels in both early- and late-harvest Greek olive oils, batches made from green early-harvest olives had nearly twice as much of the compound than oil from those picked later (however, even the oil made from late-harvest olives still had significant amounts of oleocanthal).

LESSON: Embrace extra-virgin olive oil and swap it in for less-healthy fats in your diet, such as butter. It's also worth looking for "early harvest" EVOO that has been extracted from green unripe fruit, to get the highest amount of oleocanthal and other important antioxidants. While this is not a regulated term, you can often taste the difference—the flavor will be grassy and astringent compared to regular olive oil's buttery mellowness.

Embrace the Bean and Nut

Greeks often joke that in the rocky highlands of Crete "there are more goats than Greeks." Goats were the first domestic animal the Minoans brought to the island some 3,000 years ago and are such a part of Cretan identity that the wild version of the species, known as the kri-kri, is nationally protected. Keys and Allbaugh both observed how central the goat was to island animal husbandry, and that its meat was lean and nutrient-dense. Overall, goat meat has less total fat and saturated fat, more iron and about the same amount of protein per ounce compared to beef, pork, lamb and chicken. So Cretans would have had less sat fat—which can drive up cholesterol levels—in their diets.

But the more important point from a health perspective is that even this high-quality meat was seldom on Cretan plates, according to Walter Willett, M.D., Dr.P.H., a professor of epidemiology and nutrition at Harvard University's T.H. Chan School of Public Health, who is perhaps the nation's top expert on the Mediterranean diet. Specifically, Allbaugh observed that the Cretans only ate a little over 7 ounces of goat or other red meat a week. Even fish, often imagined as a key part of this diet, was consumed in small quantities—about 6 ounces weekly. And at around 2 ounces a week, poultry was even more of a mealtime rarity. The bulk of their protein came from legumes—chickpeas, white beans, fava beans, lentils—and other types of pulses, as well as nuts, including almonds, walnuts and chestnuts. Like whole grains, beans, legumes and nuts are rich in soluble fiber and phytonutrients that may reduce the risk of various diseases, particularly when substituted for meat. The PREDIMED study reached this conclusion.

LESSON: While you probably won't find goat in your local supermarket, you can choose lean cuts of meat and eat animal proteins sparingly—Dr. Willett recommends no more than one serving a few times a month. Instead, make beans, legumes and nuts your principal protein sources.

Watch How Much You Eat—as Well as What You Eat

When Allbaugh distilled the many interviews his team did over the course of his time in Crete, the grim statement that stands out from one of his subjects was, "We are hungry most of the time." Overall intake was 2,547 calories per day—on par with average daily intake in the U.S. today. But many Cretans did backbreaking physical work every day that would necessitate many more calories than this.

Cretans also tended to spread their food out into six small meals, rather than sit down to three large ones, which many contemporary physicians recommend. A study in the *Journal of the Academy of Nutrition and Dietetics* found that people who ate at least six times a day had better overall diet quality and lower BMIs than those who ate fewer than four times daily. Other research has shown that small, frequent meals may improve cholesterol and insulin levels. Plus, Cretans observed a pattern of religious fasting that closely mirrors the 5:2 pattern of intermittent fasting that some research has shown can promote longevity and reduce blood sugar levels. In the Greek Orthodox calendar, both Wednesdays and Fridays are designated as fast days and there are also numerous religious holidays that require abstention.

LESSON: Keep calories in check and consider eating smaller, more frequent meals. You can also ask your doctor whether intermittent fasting might be right for you.

Will these seven dietary lessons from Crete turn you into a slim-waisted, super-fit individual free of heart disease and cancer—and propel you headlong into a healthy old age? Well, it could be a start. There were many factors that contributed to the longevity Allbaugh and Keys observed on Crete, including strong family and social ties, relatively low stress levels and a penchant for dancing. But for the moment, the easiest thing we can do to emulate the inhabitants of King Minos's ancient island is to change how we eat. The rest, like the basis of so much traditional Greek yogurt, is culture. ●

Paul Greenberg is the author of the James Beard Award-winning New York Times *bestseller* Four Fish, *as well as* American Catch *and* The Omega Principle.

Cook Like They Do in Crete

These recipes are inspired by the local Greek dishes found in Crete. The meals embrace the healthy tenets of the Mediterranean diet.

RECIPES BY AGLAIA KREMEZI

Dakos (Barley Rusks)

ACTIVE: 40 min **TOTAL:** 5¾ hrs
TO MAKE AHEAD: Store airtight for up to 6 months.
EQUIPMENT: Parchment paper

Malted barley grain is mainly used to brew beer and whiskey but is used here to give the rusks a sweet, nutty flavor. Look for it at home-brew stores or order it online, along with malted barley flour. Top these crunchy toasts with tomatoes, olive oil and feta or dips like taramosalata and tzatziki.

- **3 cups all-purpose flour, plus more as needed**
- **1½ cups barley flour**
- **1½ cups malted barley flour**
- **1 cup coarsely ground malted barley grain *or* malted barley flour**
- **2 tablespoons ground aniseed**
- **2 tablespoons ground coriander**
- **2 envelopes (4½ teaspoons) instant dry yeast**
- **2½ teaspoons sea salt**
- **½ teaspoon ground pepper**
- **½ cup extra-virgin olive oil plus 2 teaspoons, divided**
- **3 tablespoons grape molasses *(see Tip)* or 2 tablespoons honey plus 1 teaspoon balsamic vinegar**
- **2 cups cold water**

1. Combine all-purpose flour, barley flour, malted barley flour, malted barley grain (or more malted barley flour), aniseed, coriander, yeast, salt and pepper in the bowl of a stand mixer fitted with a dough hook. Make a well in the center and add ½ cup oil and grape molasses (or honey and vinegar). With the mixer on medium-low, add water and mix for 6 minutes. The dough should be somewhat sticky, but pull away from the sides of the bowl. If it's too dry, add a little more water; if it's too wet, add 1 to 3 tablespoons all-purpose flour.

2. Turn the dough out onto a lightly floured surface and shape into a ball. Coat a large bowl with the remaining 2 teaspoons oil, place the dough in it and turn to coat. Coat one side of a piece of plastic wrap with cooking spray and cover the bowl with it. Let the dough rise until doubled in size, 1½ to 2 hours.

3. Position racks in middle and upper thirds of oven; preheat to

400°F. Line 2 baking sheets with parchment paper.

4. Cut the dough in half and divide each half into 3 pieces. Keeping the remaining pieces covered with plastic wrap, roll one piece at a time into a thick rope, about 18 inches long. Cut in half and coil each half into a round bagel-like bun, with or without a hole in the middle. Press lightly with the heel of your hand to flatten slightly. Place the dakos about 1½ inches apart on the prepared pans. *(Alternatively, shape the dough into paximadia: Divide the dough into 4 pieces. Form each piece into a 14-inch-long log and transfer to the prepared pans.)* Cover loosely with plastic wrap and let rise for 30 minutes.

5. Bake for 10 minutes. Reduce oven temperature to 350°. Bake until firm and brown on the bottom, switching the pans from top to bottom and rotating from front to back halfway through, about 40 minutes more.

6. Reduce oven temperature to 200°. Remove the pans from the oven. Cut each dakos in half horizontally. (If you are making paximadia, let the logs cool for 5 minutes, then cut into ½-inch slices with a serrated knife.) Place the rounds (or slices) directly on the oven racks, overlapping if necessary, and bake until completely dry, about 2 hours.

7. Transfer the dakos (or paximadia) to wire racks and let cool completely, about 1 hour.

SERVES 24: 1 DAKOS OR 4 PAXIMADIA EACH
CAL 204 **FAT** 6G (SAT 1G) **CHOL** 0MG **CARBS** 34G **TOTAL SUGARS** 2G (ADDED 1G) **PROTEIN** 5G **FIBER** 4G **SODIUM** 233MG **POTASSIUM** 132MG

TIP: Find grape molasses, a syrup made from reduced grape must (freshly crushed grape juice with the skins, seeds and stems), at Middle Eastern markets or online.

Kolokythokeftedes (Baked Herb & Feta Zucchini Patties)

ACTIVE: 35 min
TOTAL: 1 hr 25 min
EQUIPMENT: Parchment paper

Greeks nibble on this popular meze in tavernas while waiting for their main courses to arrive.

- **2 pounds zucchini, shredded**
- **¾ teaspoon sea salt**
- **2 large eggs**
- **1¼ cup crumbled feta cheese (10 ounces)**
- **6 scallions, finely chopped**
- **⅔ cup finely chopped fresh dill**
- **1 tablespoon dried oregano, crumbled**
- **¼ teaspoon ground pepper**
- **1½ cups dry breadcrumbs, preferably whole wheat**
- **½ cup all-purpose flour**
- **¼ cup extra-virgin olive oil**
- **Whole-milk plain Greek yogurt for serving**

1. Toss zucchini with salt in a colander. Let stand for 20 minutes. Squeeze handfuls at a time to extract most of the moisture.

2. Preheat oven to 400°F. Line 2 baking sheets with parchment paper; coat with cooking spray.

3. Lightly beat eggs in a large bowl. Add the zucchini, feta, scallions, dill, oregano and pepper and stir gently to mix. Combine breadcrumbs and flour in a medium bowl. Mix ½ cup of the breadcrumb mixture into the zucchini mixture.

4. Shape ¼ cup of the zucchini mixture into a patty about 3 inches wide and coat in the breadcrumb mixture. Place on a prepared pan. Repeat with the remaining zucchini mixture to make 20 patties. Brush the patties with oil.

5. Bake the patties until golden brown, turning once halfway through, about 40 minutes. Serve with yogurt, if desired.

SERVES 10: 2 PATTIES EACH
CAL 229 **FAT** 14G (SAT 6G) **CHOL** 62MG **CARBS** 18G **TOTAL SUGARS** 4G (ADDED 0G) **PROTEIN** 9G **FIBER** 2G **SODIUM** 399MG **POTASSIUM** 332MG

CLOCKWISE FROM TOP RIGHT: HONDROS ME MELITZANES, REVITHIA ME KOLOKYTHA, YAHNERA.

Yahnera (Braised Greens with Lemon & Fennel)

ACTIVE: 50 min **TOTAL:** 50 min

If you prefer, instead of the croutons, you can add potatoes to the pan with the leeks, onions and fennel—and cook for about 10 minutes before adding the greens.

- **⅓ cup extra-virgin olive oil plus 2 tablespoons, divided, plus more for garnish**
- **2 large leeks, white and pale green parts only, thinly sliced and rinsed well**
- **2 medium onions, coarsely chopped**
- **1 bunch scallions, sliced**
- **1 large fennel bulb, coarsely chopped, plus ⅔ cup chopped fennel fronds or fresh dill, divided**
- **2 teaspoons fennel seeds, crushed**
- **2 pounds mixed greens, such as spinach, sorel *and/or* chard, stems trimmed and coarsely chopped**
- **½ cup water**
- **½ teaspoon salt**
- **½ teaspoon ground pepper**
- **3 cups cubed whole-wheat bread**
- **¼ cup lemon juice**

1. Heat ⅓ cup oil in a large pot over medium heat. Add leeks and cook, stirring, until soft, 5 to 10 minutes. Add onions, scallions, fennel bulb and fennel seeds; stir to coat with the oil. Add greens and cook, stirring occasionally, until wilted, 2 to 4 minutes. Stir in water, salt and pepper. Reduce heat to maintain a simmer, cover and cook until the greens are tender and most of the liquid has evaporated, about 10 minutes. (If the sauce is too watery, cook for 2 to 4 minutes over high heat to reduce it.)

2. Meanwhile, position rack in upper third of oven; preheat broiler. Spread bread on a rimmed baking sheet and toss with the remaining 2 tablespoons oil. Broil, stirring once, until crisp, 1 to 2 minutes.

3. Stir ⅓ cup fennel fronds (or dill) and lemon juice into the greens; cook for 2 minutes.

4. Serve topped with the remaining ⅓ cup fennel fronds (or dill), the croutons and more oil, if desired.

SERVES 8: 1 CUP EACH
CAL 211 **FAT** 14G (SAT 2G) **CHOL** 0MG **CARBS** 19G **TOTAL SUGARS** 5G (ADDED 0G) **PROTEIN** 5G **FIBER** 5G **SODIUM** 386MG **POTASSIUM** 790MG

Revithia me Kolokytha (Slow-Cooked Chickpeas with Orange, Lemon & Squash)

ACTIVE: 45 min **TOTAL:** 6 hrs (plus overnight soaking)

Chickpeas are commonly flavored with Seville orange, a bitter variety grown on Crete.

- **2 cups dried chickpeas**
- **¼ teaspoon baking soda**
- **⅓ cup extra-virgin olive oil, plus more for garnish**
- **2½ cups chopped onions**
- **1 tablespoon Aleppo pepper or ¾ teaspoon crushed red pepper**
- **1½ tablespoons sea salt**
- **1½ cups low-sodium vegetable broth or no-chicken broth**
- **1 cup coarsely chopped celery leaves, plus more for garnish**
- **2 4-inch strips orange zest**
- **5 cups chopped butternut squash (1-inch)**
- **¼ cup lemon juice**
- **2 tablespoons Dijon mustard**

1. Place chickpeas in a large bowl with enough cold water to cover by 3 inches. Let soak for 8 to 24 hours.

2. Preheat oven to 400°F.

3. Rinse the chickpeas. Transfer to a medium bowl and toss with baking soda.

4. Heat oil in a large ovenproof pot over medium heat. Add onions and cook, stirring occasionally, until soft, about 4 minutes. Stir in the chickpeas, Aleppo (or crushed red pepper) and salt; cook for 30 seconds. Add broth, celery leaves and orange zest. Bring to a boil over high heat, then remove from heat. Cover the pot with a double layer of foil and put the lid on.

5. Reduce oven temperature to 300°. Bake the chickpeas until very tender, about 4 hours. Stir in

squash, lemon juice and mustard; bake until the squash is tender, about 1 hour more.

6. Serve drizzled with more oil and topped with more celery leaves, if desired.

SERVES 10: 1 CUP EACH
CAL 253 **FAT** 10G (SAT 1G) **CHOL** 0MG
CARBS 34G **TOTAL SUGARS** 7G (ADDED 0G) **PROTEIN** 9G **FIBER** 9G
SODIUM 468MG **POTASSIUM** 525MG

Hondros me Melitzanes (Bulgur Pilaf with Eggplant, Pepper & Tomatoes)

ACTIVE: 35 min **TOTAL:** 50 min
EQUIPMENT: Parchment paper

On Crete, this pilaf is often made with xynohondros, or cracked wheat simmered in soured goat's milk. A sprinkling of feta pays homage to that flavor.

- **1 medium eggplant (about 1 pound), cut into 1-inch pieces**
- **3 teaspoons extra-virgin olive oil plus ½ cup, divided**
- **½ teaspoon salt, divided**
- **1½ cups coarse bulgar**
- **1½ cups chopped onion**
- **1 large green bell pepper, cut in ¼-inch pieces**
- **3 cups chopped ripe tomatoes**
- **½ cup dry white wine**
- **1½ cups water**
- **2 teaspoons Aleppo pepper or ½ teaspoon crushed red pepper**
- **1 cup crumbled feta cheese, divided**
- **½ cup chopped fresh mint, divided**

1. Preheat oven to 400°F. Line a rimmed baking sheet with parchment paper.

2. Toss eggplant with 3 tablespoons oil and ¼ teaspoon salt in a medium bowl. Spread on the prepared pan. Roast until golden, 15 to 25 minutes.

3. Meanwhile, toast bulgur in a large saucepan over medium heat, shaking the pan occasionally, until fragrant, about 5 minutes. Transfer to a bowl. Add the remaining ½ cup oil and onion to the pan. Cook, stirring occasionally, until the onion is softened, about 2 minutes. Reduce heat to medium-low, cover and cook, stirring occasionally, until the onion is very soft, 6 to 8 minutes.

4. Increase heat to medium-high and add bell pepper and the bulgur. Cook, stirring occasionally, until the bell pepper is softened, about 3 minutes. Add tomatoes and wine. Cook, stirring occasionally, for 3 minutes. Add water, Aleppo (or crushed red pepper) and the remaining ¼ teaspoon salt. Reduce heat to medium-low, cover and simmer until the bulgur is tender, 10 to 12 minutes more.

5. Remove from heat and stir in the eggplant, ½ cup feta and all but 1 tablespoon mint. Let stand, covered, for 3 minutes. Serve topped with the remaining ½ cup feta and 1 tablespoon mint.

SERVES 6: 1⅓ CUPS EACH
CAL 493 **FAT** 32G (SAT 8G) **CHOL** 22MG
CARBS 42G **TOTAL SUGARS** 8G (ADDED 0G) **PROTEIN** 10G **FIBER** 9G
SODIUM 432MG **POTASSIUM** 702MG

Aglaia Kremezi lives on the Greek island of Kea, where she teaches cooking and pens cookbooks, including The Foods of the Greek Islands.

My Big, Fat Greek Diet

In this humorous essay, an American shares her experience with the famed "healthy" Mediterranean diet: You will eat french-fry-stuffed gyros in Mykonos and doughnuts on the beach in Crete and go home with a little more (ahem) baggage than you arrived with. At least she did.

BY HELEN ELLIS

THE FIRST TIME I ATE SUPPER WITH MY HUSBAND'S relatives in Athens, it was after 10 p.m. My husband's cousin Kostas took his spot at the head of the table with two packs of cigarettes. There were three left in one pack, which he sat on top of a fresh one. He lit a cigarette, inhaled and then blew out a stream of smoke as long as the dining-room table, communicating to me (who did not speak one word of Greek) that he was going to chain-smoke throughout our meal and we were in for a long night.

His wife brought a plate of meat to the table. It was the first of many plates of meats. This plate was a pile of fried meatballs stacked higher than Marge Simpson's beehive. Then came lamb chops, pork chops, chicken-on-sticks and "sweetbreads," which with one bite I realized were not cinnamon rolls, but fried animal organs. She did not speak one word of English, but got her hospitality across with second helpings. As soon as I made a dent in my plate, our hostess forked a piece of meat to fill that hole. I was fed like this for hours. I never saw her china pattern.

I have been to Greece many times since, and after two weeks, I can't see my belt buckle. Because I *gain* weight on the *real* Mediterranean diet.

My husband bought me my first *real* gyro in Mykonos. Mykonos is an island where they *really* know how to party. When in Greece, I already eat past my bedtime, so the partying part is not for me. But I'm game for *real* food. *Real* food means authentic, and that often means: looks different, tastes delicious.

From my many visits to many malls in America, I thought I knew what a gyro was: mystery shavings off a gray cylinder of meat, twirling like a barber's pole, and stuffed into a pita, soft and warm like a potholder. Nope. A real authentic Greek gyro is indeed shaved off a spinning cylinder, but that cylinder looks like a 1970s office-desk message spike and the impaled messages are greasy slices of meat. This carnivore's merry-go-round spins in a shop's open window and glistens in the sun. The shavings do go into a pita, but the tomatoes and onions that go in, too, are the freshest you'll ever taste. How fresh? So fresh you can taste them through the garlic of the tzatziki. But here's the difference: french fries. In Greece, french fries go *inside* the sandwich.

Take a moment and digest that. When I'm in Greece, I digest gyros like mountain climbers consume Clif bars.

FYI: The only time I've had a Clif bar was when my husband made me eat one before we hiked a Cretan gorge. He said, "Helen, you have to eat this for energy. Your doughnuts aren't going to cut it."

We'd been in Crete for a few days, lolling on a beach. In my effort to beat the other hotel guests to a pair of chairs with the biggest umbrellas in the shadiest spot, I'd been bypassing the European breakfast buffet of cold ham and cheese, hard-boiled eggs, fruit, granola and Greek yogurt to stake my claim and wait to buy breakfast from the doughnut man.

Every morning at some point between 8 and 11 a.m., the doughnut man would stroll the shoreline. He carried a platter of two dozen cream-filled hot-out-of- the-fryer softball-size heaven-on-earth clouds and chanted, "DOH-NUTS! Va-neee-yah, choc-co-laht, straw-ber-eee!"

Now, all my life, my mantra has been: "A doughnut a day keeps the wrinkles away," but in Greece, I ate two a day—well, *really* two before lunch. After my sugar crash, I revived myself with a frappe. As far as I know, you can only get this type of frappe in Greece. A frappe is water, milk, sugar and Nescafé (yes, your grandma's instant coffee) shaken, not stirred, and served over ice. Shaking it gives it a 3-inch head of dense foam. Sometimes there is a machine to shake it. And sometimes a bartender with a big jelly jar. But all frappes are delicious and crammed with enough caffeine for you stay up late and learn Greek.

Specifically: how to order food.

So, when you're in Greece, may I suggest ordering *marithes tiganites,* aka "fishy fries" (fried smelt), *kolokythakia tiganita* (fried zucchini chips) and *patates tiganites* (fried potatoes).

Yes, I admit my Mediterranean diet isn't the one that doctors recommend, but it is the most real. And you can work off some of those fishy fries like my husband and I did in Crete: by hiking the Samariá Gorge for five hours.

Our tour guide warned us: Once you start, you cannot stop. Our guidebooks said if you become fatigued, there are rescue donkeys. There were NO DONKEYS!

But when we got out of the gorge, there was something. "*Mia* Mythos," I ordered. Translation: one beer.

Helen Ellis is the author of the essay collection Southern Lady Code.

COMING TOGETHER AT THE TABLE

Cyprus is a land of contrasts: jaw-dropping beauty next to the rough reality of territorial disputes. But no matter whether Turkish or Greek, food traditions are a vital part of family, identity and pride.

BY JEN ROSE SMITH

Spring cloudbursts wrap the island of Cyprus in fleeting green, softening the country's rocky cliffs, which climb high from the easternmost corner of the Mediterranean Sea. As the skies clear, residents venture out onto the cobbled streets of the capital, Nicosia, a maze of zigzag lanes framed by ancient stone fortifications. Inside the walls, pedestrians pass a jumble of elegant mosques, Byzantine churches and shuttered homes spanning centuries of history. They sip coffee at café tables alongside an obvious reminder of the country's struggles: a trail of soaked sandbags and rusting barbed wire that splits the tiny nation in two. That line mirrors the long-standing rift between the island's Greek- and Turkish-speaking communities.

When Cyprus declared independence from British rule in 1960, violence flared as the country settled into a power-sharing government between the Greek majority and Turkish minority. U.N. peacekeepers arrived in 1964, but clashes continued through another fraught decade. In 1974, the Greek military backed a government coup and troops from Turkey invaded the north days later. The Turkish forces never left, occupying one-third of the island, and today Cyprus remains divided.

Niki Psarias is striving to bridge that divide. In 2017, she started Border Kitchen, a series of events that bring islanders together for an evening of food and conversation. At the first gathering, guests pulled open the door to the Powerhouse Restaurant in Nicosia and were met with the aroma of fresh lemons, dried oregano and slow-cooked lamb. "Food brings people together," says Psarias. "We feel happy, and that helps us to be more open to new ideas."

Tahini Dip

ACTIVE: 15 min **TOTAL:** 15 min

TO MAKE AHEAD: Refrigerate for up to 2 days. Add a little water before serving if the dip is too stiff.

Super creamy with the nutty flavor of sesame seeds, this dip is a popular way to begin a meal in Cyprus. Serve with crudités and pita.

- ½ cup tahini
- 2 tablespoons lemon juice
- 1 tablespoon extra-virgin olive oil, plus more for garnish
- 1 clove garlic, crushed
- ¼ teaspoon salt
- 6 tablespoons water
- 3 tablespoons chopped fresh parsley
- Toasted sesame seeds for garnish

Combine tahini, lemon juice, oil, garlic and salt in a food processor. Pulse, scraping down the sides as needed, until smooth. With the motor running, add water in a thin stream until the mixture is pale and smooth. Transfer the dip to a serving bowl and top with parsley. Garnish with sesame seeds and more oil, if desired.

SERVES 8: 2 TBSP. EACH
CAL 106 **FAT** 10G (SAT 1G) **CHOL** 0MG **CARBS** 4G
TOTAL SUGARS 0G (ADDED 0G) **PROTEIN** 3G
FIBER 1G **SODIUM** 79MG **POTASSIUM** 82MG

Wild Asparagus with Scrambled Eggs

ACTIVE: 25 min **TOTAL:** 25 min

Spring brings a lush carpet of blooms to the hills of Cyprus and sends food-loving foragers out hunting for wild asparagus. Cooked with eggs and potatoes, it's a simple scramble that's often served as one of several small plates at dinner. You can find wild asparagus in the U.S. as well; otherwise, shop for stalks that are as young and tender as possible. (Adapted from Munevver Gurel.)

- **2 tablespoons extra-virgin olive oil, divided**
- **1 medium waxy potato, cut into ¼-inch pieces**
- **12 ounces asparagus, trimmed and cut into ¾-inch pieces**
- **½ teaspoon salt, divided**
- **4 large eggs, lightly beaten**
- **½ teaspoon ground pepper**

1. Heat 1 tablespoon oil in a medium nonstick skillet over medium heat. Add potato and cook, stirring occasionally, until golden brown, about 12 minutes. Transfer to a plate.
2. Add the remaining 1 tablespoon oil and asparagus to the pan. Cook, stirring occasionally, until the asparagus is tender, 3 to 4 minutes. Return the potato to the pan and season with ¼ teaspoon salt. Add eggs and the remaining ¼ teaspoon salt and pepper. Reduce heat to medium-low and cook, stirring occasionally, until the eggs are set, 1 to 2 minutes.

SERVES 4: ¾ CUP EACH
CAL 177 **FAT** 12G (SAT 3G) **CHOL** 186MG
CARBS 10G **TOTAL SUGARS** 2G (ADDED 0G) **PROTEIN** 8G **FIBER** 2G
SODIUM 371MG **POTASSIUM** 377MG

Black-Eyed Peas with Chard

ACTIVE: 15 min **TOTAL:** 45 min (plus overnight soaking)

Two Cypriot specialties—good olive oil and fresh lemons—lend sunny flavor to this simple bean dish, served as a side in Cyprus. Top with a dollop of Greek yogurt for a meatless main.

- **1 cup dried black-eyed peas**
- **1½ teaspoons salt, divided**
- **3 tablespoons extra-virgin olive oil, divided**
- **1 medium onion, chopped**
- **2 cloves garlic, finely chopped**
- **1 pound chard, trimmed and coarsely chopped**
- **3 cups low-sodium vegetable broth *or* no-chicken broth**
- **4 tablespoons lemon juice, divided**

1. Place black-eyed peas and 1 teaspoon salt in a medium bowl. Cover with cold water by 2 inches and soak overnight.
2. Drain and rinse the peas. Transfer to a medium saucepan with the remaining ½ teaspoon salt. Cover with 4 cups water. Bring to a boil over high heat. Reduce heat to maintain a simmer and cook until the peas are almost tender, about 15 minutes. Drain.
3. Heat 1 tablespoon oil in a large skillet over medium heat. Add onion and garlic; cook, stirring occasionally, until softened, about 3 minutes. Add chard; cook, stirring occasionally, until the greens are slightly wilted, 2 to 3 minutes more. Add the peas, broth and 2 tablespoons lemon juice. Cook, stirring occasionally, until the peas are tender, about 20 minutes.
4. Serve warm, drizzled with the remaining 2 tablespoons each oil and lemon juice.

SERVES 6: ABOUT 1 CUP EACH
CAL 186 **FAT** 8G (SAT 1G) **CHOL** 0MG
CARBS 23G **TOTAL SUGARS** 5G (ADDED 0G) **PROTEIN** 8G **FIBER** 7G
SODIUM 308MG **POTASSIUM** 543MG

Purslane, Tomato & Cucumber Salad with Mint

ACTIVE: 10 min **TOTAL:** 10 min

Purslane is a nutrient-packed green with a bright, lemony flavor and delicate crunch. Many gardeners in the U.S. consider it a weed, but Cypriots use it to make refreshing salads. If it isn't growing in your own yard, try calling a local vegetable farmer, who might be pleased to give some away, or you can order it from melissas.com *or* chefs-garden.com. *Watercress is a peppery substitute.*

- **2 tablespoons extra-virgin olive oil**
- **2 tablespoons red-wine vinegar**
- **¼ teaspoon salt**
- **3 cups trimmed purslane *or* 6 cups trimmed watercress**
- **2 medium tomatoes, diced**
- **1 medium English cucumber *or* 2 Persian (mini) cucumbers, diced**
- **2 tablespoons chopped fresh mint**

Whisk oil, vinegar and salt in a large bowl. Add purslane (or watercress), tomatoes, cucumber and mint. Toss to combine.

SERVES 5: 1 CUP EACH
CAL 73 **FAT** 6G (SAT 1G) **CHOL** 0MG
CARBS 4G **TOTAL SUGARS** 2G (ADDED 0G) **PROTEIN** 2G **FIBER** 1G
SODIUM 133MG **POTASSIUM** 350MG

FROM TOP: PURSLANE, TOMATO & CUCUMBER SALAD WITH MINT; BLACK-EYED PEAS WITH CHARD; WILD ASPARAGUS WITH SCRAMBLED EGGS

Slow-Cooked Lamb with Lemons & Pomegranate

ACTIVE: 30 min **TOTAL:** 7 hrs (including 2 hrs marinating time)

EQUIPMENT: Parchment paper

A long braise in the oven yields fork-tender results for a tough cut of lamb. Cinnamon, oregano, garlic and lemon infuse the meat with Mediterranean aromas, while a final scattering of pomegranate arils provides a burst of color and crunch.

- 2 lemons, divided
- 10 cloves garlic, divided
- 1¼ teaspoons salt, divided
- ½ teaspoon dried oregano *or* 1 teaspoon chopped fresh
- ¼ teaspoon ground cinnamon
- 1 3-pound bone-in lamb shoulder roast, trimmed
- 1 pound baby waxy potatoes
- 1 medium onion, peeled and quartered with root end intact
- 3 cups water
- ½ cup pomegranate arils
- ¼ cup chopped fresh parsley

1. Zest 1 lemon. Combine the zest, 5 garlic cloves, ¾ teaspoon salt, oregano and cinnamon in a mortar and pestle or mini food processor and blend into a paste. Rub the mixture all over lamb and place in a 5½-quart ovenproof pot with a tight-fitting lid (the lamb should fit with just a little space around the edges). Refrigerate for at least 2 hours or overnight.

2. Preheat oven to 300°F.

3. Squeeze the juice of the zested lemon over the lamb. Cut the remaining lemon in half and tuck around the lamb along with the remaining 5 garlic cloves, potatoes and onion. Pour water around the lamb in the pot.

4. Cut a piece of parchment paper a bit larger than the pot. Wet the parchment and use it to cover the lamb and vegetables, crumpling and tucking it down around the edges. Braise the lamb until fork-tender, 4 to 5 hours.

5. Discard the parchment. Increase oven temperature to 425°F. Baste the lamb with the pan juices and continue cooking until the top is browned, 10 to 15 minutes more.

6. Cover the pot and let stand for 15 minutes. Transfer the lamb to a serving platter along with the potatoes, onion and garlic. Sprinkle with pomegranate arils and parsley before serving.

SERVES 8: 3 OZ. LAMB AND ½ CUP VEGETABLES & SAUCE EACH
CAL 385 **FAT** 23G (SAT 9G) **CHOL** 111MG **CARBS** 14G **TOTAL SUGARS** 3G (ADDED 0G) **PROTEIN** 30G **FIBER** 2G **SODIUM** 449MG **POTASSIUM** 588MG

GROWN IN PUGLIA

From fava, artichokes, eggplant and broccoli rabe to some of the best seafood in the country, the heel of the boot is Italy's breadbasket. Here's how it mastered the real Mediterranean diet.

BY JANE BLACK

"What do you do with these?" I asked, pointing to a bunch of what looked like the prettiest wild asparagus I had ever seen. The stems were a vivid cherry color, and the delicate purple stalks were laced with feathery green leaves. "Ah, *cicoria rossa*," the market vendor answered—red chicory. He was a stout man with a buzz of silver hair and lively blue eyes, and he seemed pleased that this bunch of Americans were genuinely interested in the local cuisine. Here in the hill town of Martina Franca in Puglia, he explained, the locals boil chicory and serve it with young fava beans. But in his village, they chop it, boil it and toss it with pasta. "They would never do that here," he said, wagging a thick finger at us.

His village was six miles away.

And so it is in Puglia, the heel of Italy's boot, where the food and the culinary traditions put to shame Americans' notion of what counts as local. While we pat ourselves on

the back for even knowing what's in season, Puglians almost exclusively use ingredients grown no more than a few miles from home, whether it's the hard durum wheat for their pasta or tomatoes, eggplant, figs or olives. They prepare things the same way their mothers and grandmothers did, which may be quite different from the way someone else's *nonna* did. And you find the valley's signature dish, orecchiette with broccoli rabe, only six months a year, when local broccoli rabe is in season.

But everything seems to grow here: grapes for wine, artichokes and almonds, cherries and tomatoes, and cabbage and broccoli, which in the fall sprout in stony fields beneath the olive trees. The region's hundreds of miles of coast bring locals sardines, snapper, mussels and anchovies.

Like that of many Americans, my first experience in Italy was in Tuscany. I studied at the University of Florence, found the requisite Italian boyfriend and dined on bistecca alla fiorentina and Chianti. Then, 10 years ago, I made my first trip to Puglia, and I'd wanted to go back ever since. There was something wild—something real—that was missing in Italy's other stopped-in-time, touristy destinations. Unmortared stone walls march unevenly across the fields, like drunken soldiers lackadaisically guarding their trulli, the mystical round houses topped with conical stone roofs. The locals seem genuinely happy to meet and help you; once, hopelessly lost while driving, I asked a professorial man for directions. Rather than try to explain, he hopped on his bike and led me to the gates of the city.

Puglia has since been "discovered" by chefs and tourists. But I was pleased, when I finally returned a few years ago with a friend, to find it as unspoiled as I remembered. The olive trees, set in walled orchards, had hulking, gnarled trunks and halos of silver shimmering leaves. There was a breakfast of frittata with zucchini and mint, rustic bread and homemade fig preserves served in the dappled shade of a grape arbor. A lunch of grilled sardines, roasted potatoes and bitter greens while overlooking the sea. Life went on as it always has: In front of the houses, people set out wooden boards in the sun to dry herbs, figs and tomatoes. And it wasn't unusual to see an elderly man or woman scrambling down a hillside to gather wild chicory.

The fantasy-fulfilling food bursting from this lush setting had me itching to get into the kitchen, so I asked chef and instructor Domenico Maggi to give me Pugliese cooking lessons at his family's home. In his outdoor kitchen, Mino, as everyone calls him, showed me how he makes pasta dough by mixing locally milled whole-grain flour with a handful of semolina and water. After rolling out small pieces of the dough into long snakes with his hands, he snips off pieces and forms orecchiette ("little ear" shapes) over his thumb. The whole-grain pasta stands up to the strong flavors of the anchovies, the garlic and the bitter broccoli rabe that are its classic pairing. It's also what his mother used. "White flour was special; it was the kind of thing you gave to the doctor or the priest as a gift," he remembers. "I've always liked whole grains. But I have become more and more convinced over time that they are part of the real Mediterranean diet."

Mino grew up in the rolling hills of the southwestern part of the region during the 1950s and '60s, a time when many Puglians were still fleeing the region's poverty for America. The family didn't get electricity until he was 7, and even after that, his mother continued to cook everything in a wood-fired oven. The family's meals were simple. They ate fava beans and chicory, baked eggplant and zucchini, and everything was cooked with plenty of extra-virgin olive oil. At every meal, there was a bowl of raw vegetables on the table to provide vitamins and to aid digestion. The tradition continues today, both at home and in restaurants, where an elegant bowl of whatever is seasonal—shaved radishes or fennel or sweet carrots—is served with the antipasti or, just as often, over ice before dessert.

A few days after my Puglian cooking lessons, my friend and I took the winding road from Martina Franca along the Adriatic coast to Monopoli, a fishing port with a gracious and hidden historical center. We waited with friends for nearly an hour for a table at Osteria Perricci, where there is no menu because the kitchen only serves whatever looks best that day. For us, that included grilled shrimp, mackerel marinated in vinegar and mint, cold salads of tender octopus and squid, pasta with mussels, whole roasted sea bass and, of course, a plate of fresh vegetables.

"How was everything?" the signora asked us as we finished our meal with a much-needed bay leaf *digestivo*.

We answered in a chorus: *Buonissimo!* Amazing! *Fantastico!*

"Just as it has always been," added one of our friends, who has been eating at Osteria Perricci for 20 years.

"Good," the signora said. "Just as it should be." ●

Buon Appetito

If you're dreaming of southern Italy's local favorites, try these healthy and delicious recipes at home.

Fava Bean Puree with Chicory

ACTIVE: 20 min
TOTAL: 1 hr 25 min

This dish exemplifies the simplicity of the region's cuisine. Wild or cultivated chicory is often served raw or cooked, as it is here, with a simple puree of fava beans seasoned solely with olive oil and salt. If you have a special olive oil in your pantry, this is the time to pull it out.

- **8 ounces skinless dried fava beans (about 1½ cups)**
- **1 small red potato, peeled and sliced**
- **1 tablespoon extra-virgin olive oil, plus more for serving**
- **½ teaspoon salt plus 2 teaspoons, divided**
- **2 pounds chicory *or* curly endive (from 2 bunches), trimmed**

1. Place beans and potato in a medium saucepan; add water to cover by ½ inch. Bring to a boil over high heat, skimming off any foam that rises to the surface. Reduce heat to maintain a gentle simmer, cover and cook, stirring occasionally, until the mixture is a thick, soupy consistency, about 1 hour.

2. Transfer the bean mixture to a blender. Add 1 tablespoon oil and ½ teaspoon salt; puree until smooth. Transfer to a platter (or bowl).

3. Put a large pot of water on to boil.

4. Wash chicory (or endive) in a large bowl of water to remove any grit. Stir the remaining 2 teaspoons salt into the boiling water, then add the greens and cook, stirring occasionally, until tender, 6 to 8 minutes. Drain in a colander, pressing to remove excess water.

5. Serve the greens with the fava bean puree, drizzled with a little olive oil, if desired.

SERVES 6: ABOUT ⅔ CUP GREENS & ½ CUP PUREE EACH
CAL 203 **FAT** 3G (SAT 1G) **CHOL** 0MG **CARBS** 33G **TOTAL SUGARS** 3G (ADDED 0G) **PROTEIN** 13G **FIBER** 16G **SODIUM** 407MG **POTASSIUM** 1,105MG

Stuffed Fresh Sardines

ACTIVE: 50 min
TOTAL: 50 min

When you dine in one of the towns peppered along Puglia's nearly 500 miles of coastline, expect to see fish served in simple preparations, like these fried stuffed sardines.

- **¼ cup part-skim ricotta cheese**
- **¼ cup finely shredded Pecorino Romano cheese**
- **¼ cup fresh breadcrumbs**
- **¼ cup chopped fresh parsley**
- **3 large eggs, divided**
- **Zest of 1 lemon, plus lemon wedges for serving**
- **½ teaspoon salt, divided**
- **½ teaspoon ground pepper, divided**
- **12 medium fresh sardines, gutted, head and tail left on**
- **½ cup all-purpose flour**
- **2 cups panko breadcrumbs**
- **1½ cups extra-virgin olive oil**

1. Combine ricotta, Romano, fresh breadcrumbs, parsley, 1 egg, lemon zest and ¼ teaspoon each salt and pepper in a medium bowl.

2. Rinse sardines and pat dry. Season the insides with the remaining ¼ teaspoon each salt and pepper. Stuff each sardine with about 2 teaspoons of the cheese mixture.

3. Place flour in one shallow dish, the remaining 2 eggs (lightly beaten) in a second shallow dish and panko in a third dish. Dip the sardines in the flour, then the egg, then the panko.

4. Heat oil in a large cast-iron skillet over medium-high heat until shimmering but not smoking. Fry the sardines, in batches, until golden brown, 2 to 4 minutes per side, reducing the heat as needed. Serve immediately, with lemon wedges.

SERVES 6: 2 STUFFED SARDINES EACH
CAL 420 **FAT** 26G (SAT 5G)
CHOL 170MG **CARBS** 19G
TOTAL SUGARS 1G (ADDED 0G)
PROTEIN 26G **FIBER** 1G **SODIUM** 423MG **POTASSIUM** 366MG

CHAPTER 3

EVERYDAY MEDITERRANEAN

You don't need to live steps from the sea to reap the benefits of this healthy eating plan. Here are strategies and recipes to embrace more of the good-for-you Mediterranean elements in your day-to-day.

THE ULTIMATE MEDITERRANEAN DIET SHOPPING LIST

Stock your kitchen with these minimally processed foods that promote the world's healthiest dietary pattern.

JAMIE VESPA, M.S., R.D.

The Mediterranean diet is far from novel. The centuries-old way of eating is native to the countries surrounding the Mediterranean Sea; however, it's only become the subject of scientific nutrition deep-dives in the last 50 or so years.

A great body of evidence shows that this way of eating—brimming with plant-based foods, healthy fats, lean proteins, whole grains and moderate amounts of wine, may help you live longer and stave off chronic diseases, such as cardiovascular disease and diabetes. One key component of the Mediterranean diet is the emphasis on foods that may thwart inflammation and oxidative stress, which is at the root of many chronic diseases. These foods include omega-3-rich fish, fruits and vegetables, nuts and seeds, and healthy oils. The dietary pattern is particularly rich in monounsaturated fats, which can help decrease bad LDL cholesterol and raise good HDL cholesterol—a win-win for the cardiovascular system. Plus, the heightened emphasis on plant-based foods ensures a bounty of fiber and phytonutrients.

The prominence of plant foods in the Mediterranean diet leaves little room for processed foods, added sugar and saturated fat. And although full-fat dairy is still consumed in moderation, red meat and sweets are limited to a few times per month.

At its core, the culinary landscape around the Mediterranean diet is quite simple. It hinges on preparing fresh, seasonal foods simply to let the quality and inherent taste of each ingredient shine. Read on for a list of Mediterranean must-haves.

Extra-Virgin Olive Oil

Varying dietary patterns make up the overall Mediterranean diet, but olive oil is at the core of each one. Extra-virgin olive oil is rich in tocopherols, carotenoids and polyphenols, giving it antioxidant and anti-inflammatory properties. This kitchen staple is as versatile in cooking as it is for everyday staples, such as dips, spreads and salad dressings.

Fresh Fruits and Veggies

Fresh, locally sourced, seasonal produce takes center stage in Mediterranean cuisine. Dark leafy greens such as kale, beet greens, mustard greens and collard greens are often added to frittatas, beans and lentil soups. Wild greens like rocket, chicory and dandelion are also popular in both cooked and raw dishes. Other vegetables common to this region include artichokes, beets, broccoli, cucumber, eggplant, mushrooms, radishes and onions. Garlic, in particular, is a mainstay in Mediterranean cooking; it's used as a versatile flavor agent in everything from sauces and soups to grain dishes (and it packs some impressive health benefits).

Fruits common to the Mediterranean diet include apples, apricots, avocados, berries, citrus, dates, figs, grapes, stone fruit and pomegranates. Lemons are often used to squeeze over fish, veggies, soups and beans for a fresh finish.

Fresh Herbs and Spices

Aromatic herbs and spices are staples in Mediterranean cooking. These plant-based seasoning agents reduce the need to add excess salt, plus they provide a range of antioxidants that promote health. Each region in the Mediterranean has different flavor preferences; however, you can count on parsley, basil, oregano, coriander and bay leaves to make frequent appearances. Use fresh basil to make homemade pesto, or a bunch of parsley to form the base of a zesty gremolata.

Fresh and Canned Seafood

Fish and shellfish are key sources of protein and healthy fats in the Mediterranean diet. Omega-3–rich fish such as tuna, sardines and salmon are enjoyed fresh or canned. Mussels, clams and shrimp are often featured in pasta and grain dishes, or simply served with lemon, olive oil and herbs. Most Mediterranean patterns encourage seafood consumption twice per week.

Whole Grains

Wheat is the foundation grain of the Mediterranean. Farro is one of the traditional grains used in both hot dishes and cold salads in Italy. Another classic grain is bulgur, which is made from cracked wheat berries and used in pilafs and tabbouleh. Couscous, pasta and barley are also commonly found in different regions. When shopping for whole grains, look for the term "whole" or "whole grain" on the front of the package and in the ingredient list—it should be the first ingredient listed.

Legumes (Dried and Canned)

One of the most prevalent pulses in Mediterranean cuisine is the chickpea, which is whipped into hummus, formed in falafel and tossed into salads. Lentils are also commonly used in soups and stews for tasty one-pot meals packed with fiber and protein. Black-eyed peas, kidney beans and cannellini beans are often tossed into salads with a drizzle of olive oil and a fresh squeeze of lemon.

Nuts and Seeds

Nuts and seeds are enjoyed as a satisfying snack thanks to their trifecta of fiber, protein and fat. A common condiment on the coastline of the Mediterranean is tahini, which is made from ground sesame seeds. Most famously used in hummus, this versatile condiment also makes salad dressings sing. Use it in sauces or dressings to spoon over roasted veggies or grain bowls.

Olives and Capers

Table olives are enjoyed as a simple snack, or to complement a tray of crudités. Kalamata olives are among the most popular and are often tossed into Greek salads and pasta or blitzed into a tapenade. Olives are rich sources of antioxidant polyphenols and heart-healthy fats. Brined or dried, capers are praised for their briny bite and the way they effortlessly punch up the flavor of pasta, baked fish and dressings.

Canned Tomatoes

Whole, diced, stewed or concentrated into a paste, both canned and fresh tomatoes are everyday staples in the Mediterranean. Canned tomato products are particularly rich in lycopene (due to the heating process), which may help protect against certain cancers. A few tomato-centric staples in the Mediterranean include shakshuka, stuffed tomatoes, baked fish with tomatoes, and, of course, marinara sauce.

Greek Yogurt and Artisanal Cheeses

The Mediterranean diet encourages savoring small amounts of full-fat dairy, alongside plenty of fruits, vegetables and whole grains. In addition to providing extra protein to plant-centric meals, yogurt is fermented and rich in gut-healthy probiotics. This region spotlights traditionally cultured cheeses (made from milk and natural cultures), as opposed to some of the more processed varieties commonly available in the U.S.

Beyond being used in the classic Greek salad, feta cheese often accompanies stews and fish dishes. Halloumi cheese is known for its firm texture, which makes it suitable for grilling and frying. Harder cheeses like Pecorino Romano and Parmigiano-Reggiano are often grated into pasta, while manchego can be baked into egg dishes.

Red Wine

Wine is a common accompaniment to Mediterranean meals, but it's generally consumed in moderation (a 5-ounce pour is the standard). Red wine, in particular, contains antioxidant polyphenols and the flavonoid resveratrol, which may help increase HDL cholesterol and decrease LDL cholesterol levels. ●

HOW TO CHOOSE THE BEST SEAFOOD

Inspired by regions on the coast, the Mediterranean diet is loaded with seafood options. Here's how you can make healthy, affordable and sustainable choices.

BY KORSHA WILSON

When the Mediterranean diet burst into America's national consciousness in the 1970s, it promoted adding healthy fats to our diets in the form of glugs of olive oil and encouraged eschewing meat-focused dishes in favor of meals heavy on hearty legumes, herbs, spices and lots of fresh vegetables. The diet's major selling point is that it highlights foods commonly eaten by people who live in the Mediterranean, a group of people, studies have shown, who live longer, happier lives than groups in other parts of the world.

Given the region it uses as inspiration and the fact that much of the land there touches the Mediterranean Sea, seafood plays a big part in a modern Mediterranean diet. The immense variety of finned fish, shrimp and mussels in the waters are a key part of many meals there and the sea a big part of outdoor life. (There's a reason Poseidon, the god of the sea, is one of the most

powerful gods in Greek mythology.)

"In addition to providing essential good fats, seafood is packed with protein that contributes to a healthy diet, and most people would benefit from incorporating seafood as a protein option," says Kelly Toups, director of nutrition for Oldways, an organization dedicated to "helping people live healthier, happier lives through cultural food traditions." If you're not getting enough protein, adding more of it to your diet has been shown to keep you full longer and aid in muscle development, but with seafood, the benefits don't stop there. Studies have shown that seafood is great for the health of expectant mothers and the cognitive development of young children too. "The research consistently shows that regular seafood consumption before and during pregnancy can help lower pregnancy complications," Toups says, citing a 2020 report released by the Dietary Guidelines for Americans advisory committee, which found that seafood intake was beneficial to children and adolescents. Heart health is also impacted. "Eating approximately one to two 3-ounce servings of fatty fish per week, like salmon or sardines, reduces the risk of dying from heart disease by 36%," Toups says.

Eating two servings a week of fatty fish was also linked to decreased Alzheimer's disease pathology, she adds. But while seafood itself is healthy, the way it's prepared can also impact the health benefits. "Instead of battered and deep-fried seafood, try to look for grilled or roasted options," says Toups. "Or instead of seafood that's served in a creamy sauce or a butter sauce, pick an option that's prepared with olive oil or citrus."

For pregnant and soon-to-be-pregnant women, the FDA cautions against fish with higher levels of mercury, which include larger fish like swordfish, king mackerel and shark. Smaller fish and crustaceans, such as shrimp and scallops, ingest less mercury over their lifetimes.

WE MIGHT NOT ALL BE LUCKY ENOUGH TO LIVE ON a sun-soaked Greek isle or on the coast, but incorporating seafood into our diets can have incredible health benefits and even help improve the ocean's ecosystem. But how can shoppers in landlocked locales incorporate this superfood into their lives in a way that's sustainable while making sure the seafood remains high quality?

Ryan Bigelow, a senior program manager at Seafood Watch, advises consumers to do their research into what's available in their area and what to avoid so that they can stick to seafood that provides optimal health benefits without harming the environment. "There are always exceptions, but as a general rule of thumb, avoid bluefin tuna and eel," he says, citing overfishing.

Overfishing means fish are caught at a rate that's faster than they can reproduce, leading to marine ecosystem imbalance, which causes a decrease in certain fish species. Asking your local fishmonger or the person working the seafood counter at your grocery store about what's on offer and why is also a good option. "A lot of people ask me, 'What can my role be to help protect the ocean?' And what I tell them is, 'Ask questions,'" Bigelow says.

Being flexible by adapting your recipes to include fish that are native to your area is also a good way to make more eco-friendly choices. "Don't be shy about asking the person behind the fish for recommendations," Toups says. If the recipe you're making calls for haddock and you can't find it at your local fish counter, look for flounder or even catfish, or ask which fish would make a good substitute. "They have a lot of knowledge about the different types of fish that they have out, so asking 'What do you recommend instead?' can be really helpful," she adds.

Great sustainable seafood options can also be found in the canned and frozen sections of your grocery store. "These days it's really easy to find seafood that has been flash frozen into fillets," Toups says. "I would say that both frozen seafood and canned seafood can definitely be great options and honestly are a lot easier for families to implement into their diet." The labels on canned and frozen seafood can give you a sense of where the product is from and whether any salt or solution was added, she adds. "Comparing labels is key to make sure there's not added salt or, with canned seafood, seeing if it's canned in oil versus water."

Today, canned seafood goes beyond tuna and salmon. Mackerel, sardines, trout and even mussels are widely available, packed in water or oil. Oil-packed provides a lot of flavor, but the actual seafood absorbs oil, leading to a higher calorie count. Water-packed is a lower-calorie alternative. And don't assume that just because seafood is frozen or canned that it can't be high quality, Bigelow says. For example, a lot of fish used for sashimi is flash frozen to "maintain its freshness and kill parasites." Labels will also let you know if the product has been certified by Seafood Watch as sustainable. Seafood Watch recommends looking for descriptions like "pole-caught," "troll-caught" or "pole and line caught" on canned items like tuna and salmon. "You can have sustainable canned products, frozen products, fresh products, all those things are possible," says Bigelow.

The labels on both canned and frozen seafood can give you a sense of where the product is from and whether any salt or solution was added.

Asking questions is likewise important when you're at a restaurant or researching where to go out for a meal. Many restaurants will list whether a fish is local and share their commitment to sustainability on their websites. If you're already at dinner, you can ask your server where the seafood is from. "If you don't know what their commitment is to sustainable seafood and you can't find out the information you need, then a vegetarian option might be a more sustainable option," Bigelow says.

Another way to add high-quality seafood to your diet (and know where it's coming from) is to build relationships with local fishermen by looking into community supported fisheries (CSFs). Many people are familiar with CSAs, or community supported agriculture, in which customers pay for seasonal shares of produce directly from farms, but most people don't know that local fisheries offer programs that work the same way.

Brett Tolley, the national program coordinator for the Northwest Atlantic Marine Alliance (NAMA), grew up in Cape Cod, Massachusetts, in a family of fishermen. His family relied on only a few seafood buyers, nearly all the catch was exported, and the local community lost much of its access to locally caught seafood. Today he works to support a national Local Catch Network of fishermen and consumers to build a more transparent seafood supply chain, including connecting consumers to their closest CSF. NAMA's Local Catch Network offers a list of retailers and fish markets where consumers can find offerings from reputable sources.

The site also lists CSFs nationwide that provides customers with a weekly or monthly share of fresh, local seafood that can be picked up either at the dock or at a designated location. And if those options aren't possible, just try to buy as local as possible. "Choices can be limited depending on geography but also depending on income," Tolley says. "We advise people to avoid industrial seafood and farmed salmon whenever possible and buy fish from small- and medium-scale businesses who know the boat where the fish came from."

Tolley says one of the best ways to be sure about the quality of the seafood that you're buying is to ask how it was caught or produced. "We try to make a distinction around scale and differentiating between community-based scale versus industrial scale," he explains. It's a best bet to avoid farmed options of salmon and shrimp and to buy from small and medium companies rather than multinational seafood companies, whose fish may have traveled for thousands of miles to get to your grocery store.

It might seem overwhelming to think about all of these things when you're standing at your seafood counter, but organizations like Seafood Watch, run by Monterey Bay Aquarium, have created resource guides for all 50 states to help consumers make the best choices. Seafood Watch's website offers nearly 2,000 recommendations and provides downloadable consumer guides categorizing seafood into best choices, alternatives and species to avoid.

The site even includes a national guide listing best choices for fish farmed in the United States, like catfish, arctic char, squid, scallops and rockfish. The guide also lists fish consumers should avoid at all costs—like shark, orange roughy, tilapia from China, yellowfin tuna and spiny lobsters from South America.

+ LOOK FOR SARDINES WITH SKIN AND BONES (WHICH ARE EDIBLE), SINCE THEY HAVE MORE THAN FOUR TIMES THE AMOUNT OF CALCIUM AS SKINLESS, BONELESS SARDINES.

Bigelow, who helped create the guides, uses them himself when shopping, by accessing the Seafood Watch app on this phone. "I have my phone out when I go shopping, and I start with that list, then I look for eco certification," he says. For each option on the "best choices," "good alternatives" and "avoid" lists, there's also information about fishing methods and origin points to avoid or support so consumers can make more educated choices in the future. Fish caught using the trawl method, for example, means it was most likely caught by a large commercial fishing boat using large nets that were designed to catch as many fish as possible but can damage coral reefs and catch fish species that are endangered.

Seafood Watch takes these factors into consideration when determining if it recommends that consumers avoid certain species, since trawl fishing can be just as harmful as overfishing, because it impacts the ocean's biodiversity and the communities that depend on the oceans for a major part of their diet. "Simply put, we're looking at what is the impact of this operation on the environment and can it be continued into the future," Bigelow says.

And remember that your choices as a consumer impact not only health but also your local waterways; your choices can help create a healthier ocean. Seafood Watch is dedicated to conserving the ocean, says Bigelow. "At the heart of that is developing recommendations, doing hard science on what makes up a sustainable fishery or farm, and then taking that information and communicating it again to businesses, chefs, consumers and everyone in between." And consumers' choices play a big part in that too. "Remember your most powerful tool and the best thing you can do for the ocean is to share your voice," Bigelow says. ●

14 MEDITERRANEAN DINNERS

Make one of these dinners each night for two weeks, and you'll be well on your way to Mediterranean diet success. From colorful sheet-pan recipes to veggie-packed pastas, these meals are both healthy and delicious.

Charred Shrimp & Pesto Buddha Bowls

ACTIVE: 25 min **TOTAL:** 25 min

These shrimp and pesto Buddha bowls are delicious, healthy and pretty, and they take less than 30 minutes to prep. In other words, they're basically the ultimate easy weeknight dinner. Feel free to add other vegetables and swap the shrimp for chicken, steak, tofu or edamame.

- ⅓ cup prepared pesto
- 2 tablespoons balsamic vinegar
- 1 tablespoon extra-virgin olive oil
- ½ teaspoon salt
- ¼ teaspoon ground pepper
- 1 pound peeled and deveined large shrimp (16-20 count), patted dry
- 4 cups arugula
- 2 cups cooked quinoa
- 1 cup halved cherry tomatoes
- 1 avocado, diced

1. Whisk pesto, vinegar, oil, salt and pepper in a large bowl. Remove 4 tablespoons of the mixture to a small bowl; set both bowls aside.

2. Heat a large cast-iron skillet over medium-high heat. Add shrimp and cook, stirring, until just cooked through with a slight char, 4 to 5 minutes. Remove to a plate.

3. Add arugula and quinoa to the large bowl with the vinaigrette and toss to coat. Divide the arugula mixture among 4 bowls. Top with tomatoes, avocado and the shrimp. Drizzle each bowl with 1 tablespoon of the reserved pesto mixture.

SERVES 4: 2½ CUPS EACH

CAL 429 **FAT** 22G (SAT 4G) **CHOL** 188MG **CARBS** 29G **TOTAL SUGARS** 5G **PROTEIN** 31G **FIBER** 7G **SODIUM** 571MG **POTASSIUM** 901MG

Chicken with Tomato-Balsamic Pan Sauce

ACTIVE: 35 min **TOTAL:** 35 min

Fennel seeds give this tomato and balsamic sauce an extra kick, but if you don't have them on hand, try using cumin or coriander seeds, or 1 teaspoon of a ground herb or spice. Serve this easy chicken breast recipe with whole-wheat spaghetti or crusty bread to sop up the sauce. Save the unused chicken tenders in an airtight container in your freezer for up to 3 months. Once you have enough, thaw them out for another use.

- **2 8-ounce boneless, skinless chicken breasts**
- **½ teaspoon salt, divided**
- **½ teaspoon ground pepper, divided**
- **¼ cup white whole-wheat flour**
- **3 tablespoons extra-virgin olive oil, divided**
- **½ cup halved cherry tomatoes**
- **2 tablespoons sliced shallot**
- **¼ cup balsamic vinegar**
- **1 cup low-sodium chicken broth**
- **1 tablespoon minced garlic**
- **1 tablespoon fennel seeds, toasted and lightly crushed**
- **1 tablespoon butter**

1. Remove and reserve chicken tenders (if attached) for another use. Slice each breast in half horizontally to make 4 pieces total. Place on a cutting board and cover with a large piece of plastic wrap. Pound with the smooth side of a meat mallet or a heavy saucepan to an even thickness of about ¼ inch. Sprinkle with ¼ teaspoon each salt and pepper. Place flour in a shallow dish and dredge the cutlets to coat both sides, shaking off excess. (Discard remaining flour.)

2. Heat 2 tablespoons oil in a large skillet over medium-high heat. Add 2 pieces of chicken and cook, turning once, until evenly browned and cooked through, 2 to 3 minutes per side. Transfer to a large serving plate and tent with foil to keep warm. Repeat with the remaining chicken.

3. Add the remaining 1 tablespoon oil, tomatoes and shallot to the pan. Cook, stirring occasionally, until softened, 1 to 2 minutes. Add vinegar; bring to a boil. Cook, scraping up any browned bits from the bottom of the pan, until the vinegar is reduced by about half, about 45 seconds. Add broth, garlic, fennel seeds and the remaining ¼ teaspoon salt and pepper. Cook, stirring, until the sauce is reduced by about half, 4 to 7 minutes. Remove from heat; stir in butter. Serve the sauce over the chicken.

SERVES 4: 3 OZ. CHICKEN & 3 TBSP. SAUCE EACH
CAL 294 **FAT** 17G (SAT 4G) **CHOL** 70MG **CARBS** 10G
TOTAL SUGARS 3G (ADDED 0G) **PROTEIN** 25G
FIBER 2G **SODIUM** 371MG **POTASSIUM** 363MG

Cheesy Spinach & Artichoke Stuffed Spaghetti Squash

ACTIVE: 25 min **TOTAL:** 25 min

This spaghetti-squash-for-pasta swap slashes both carbs and calories by 75 percent for a delicious, creamy casserole you can feel good about eating. It's worth roasting the squash versus cooking it in the microwave if you have the time: The flavor gets sweeter and more intense.

- **1 2½- to 3-pound spaghetti squash, cut in half lengthwise and seeds removed**
- **3 tablespoons water, divided**
- **1 5-ounce package baby spinach**
- **1 cup (10-ounce package) frozen artichoke hearts, thawed and chopped**
- **4 ounces reduced-fat cream cheese, cubed and softened**
- **½ cup grated Parmesan cheese, divided**
- **¼ teaspoon salt**
- **¼ teaspoon ground pepper**
- **Crushed red pepper and chopped fresh basil for garnish**

1. Place squash cut-side down in a microwave-safe dish; add 2 tablespoons water. Microwave, uncovered, on High until tender, 10 to 15 minutes. *(Alternatively, place squash halves cut-side down on a rimmed baking sheet. Bake at 400°F until tender, 40 to 50 minutes.)*

2. Meanwhile, combine spinach and the remaining 1 tablespoon water in a large skillet over medium heat. Cook, stirring occasionally, until wilted, 3 to 5 minutes. Drain and transfer to a large bowl.

3. Position rack in upper third of oven; preheat broiler.

4. Use a fork to scrape the squash from the shells into the bowl. Place the shells on a baking sheet. Stir artichoke hearts, cream cheese, ¼ cup Parmesan, salt and pepper into the squash mixture. Divide it between the squash shells and top with the remaining ¼ cup Parmesan. Broil until the cheese is golden brown, about 3 minutes. Sprinkle with crushed red pepper and basil, if desired.

SERVES 4: 1¼ CUPS EACH
CAL 223 **FAT** 11G (SAT 6G) **CHOL** 28MG **CARBS** 23G **TOTAL SUGARS** 7G (ADDED 0G) **PROTEIN** 10G **FIBER** 9G **SODIUM** 528MG **POTASSIUM** 482MG

Greek Burgers with Herb-Feta Sauce

ACTIVE: 25 min **TOTAL:** 25 min

These healthy burgers get a Mediterranean twist with a yogurt sauce seasoned with oregano, lemon and feta cheese. If you can't find ground lamb, ask the butcher to grind some for you.

- **1 cup nonfat plain Greek yogurt**
- **¼ cup crumbled feta cheese**
- **3 tablespoons chopped fresh oregano, divided**
- **¼ teaspoon lemon zest**
- **2 teaspoons lemon juice**
- **¾ teaspoon salt, divided**
- **1 small red onion**
- **1 pound ground lamb *or* ground beef**
- **½ teaspoon ground pepper**
- **2 whole-wheat pitas, halved, split and warmed**
- **1 cup sliced cucumber**
- **1 plum tomato, sliced**

1. Preheat grill to medium-high or preheat broiler to high.

2. Mix yogurt, feta, 1 tablespoon oregano, lemon zest, lemon juice and ¼ teaspoon salt in a small bowl.

3. Cut ¼-inch-thick slices of onion to make ¼ cup. Finely chop more onion to make ¼ cup. (Reserve any remaining onion for another use.) Mix the chopped onion and meat in a large bowl with the remaining 2 tablespoons oregano and ½ teaspoon each salt and pepper. Form into 4 oval patties, about 4 inches by 3 inches.

4. Grill or broil the burgers, turning once, until an instant-read thermometer registers 160°F, 4 to 6 minutes per side. Serve in pita halves, with the sauce, onion slices, cucumber and tomato.

SERVES 4: 1 BURGER EACH
CAL 375 **FAT** 18G (SAT 8G) **CHOL** 86MG
CARBS 23G **TOTAL SUGARS** 4G (ADDED 0G)
PROTEIN 30G **FIBER** 3G **SODIUM** 775MG
POTASSIUM 510MG

Greek Stuffed Portobello Mushrooms

ACTIVE: 15 min **TOTAL:** 25 min

A mixture of tomatoes, spinach, feta, olives and fresh oregano gives portobellos a Mediterranean vibe in this healthy stuffed mushroom recipe. Serve these along with chicken, fish or tofu as a super-satisfying side dish, or add a hearty salad and make the portobellos the centerpiece of a vegetarian dinner.

- 3 tablespoons extra-virgin olive oil, divided
- 1 clove garlic, minced
- ½ teaspoon ground pepper, divided
- ¼ teaspoon salt
- 4 portobello mushrooms (about 14 ounces), wiped clean, stems and gills removed
- 1 cup chopped spinach
- ½ cup quartered cherry tomatoes
- ⅓ cup crumbled feta cheese
- 2 tablespoons pitted and sliced Kalamata olives
- 1 tablespoon chopped fresh oregano

1. Preheat oven to 400°F.

2. Combine 2 tablespoons oil, garlic, ¼ teaspoon pepper and salt in a small bowl. Using a silicone brush, coat mushrooms all over with the oil mixture. Place on a large rimmed baking sheet and bake until the mushrooms are mostly soft, 8 to 10 minutes.

3. Meanwhile, combine spinach, tomatoes, feta, olives, oregano and the remaining 1 tablespoon oil in a medium bowl. Once the mushrooms have softened, remove from the oven and fill with the spinach mixture. Bake until the tomatoes have wilted, about 10 minutes.

SERVES 4: 1 STUFFED MUSHROOM EACH
CAL 151 **FAT** 9G (SAT 3G) **CHOL** 11MG **CARBS** 7G
TOTAL SUGARS 4G (ADDED 0G) **PROTEIN** 5G **FIBER** 2G
SODIUM 390MG **POTASSIUM** 467MG

Mediterranean Stuffed Chicken Breasts

ACTIVE: 25 min **TOTAL:** 1 hr

Browning the chicken in a skillet before baking gives it a beautiful golden color, and finishing it in the oven ensures that this healthy baked chicken recipe cooks evenly throughout.

- ½ cup crumbled feta cheese
- ½ cup chopped roasted bell peppers
- ½ cup chopped fresh spinach
- ¼ cup Kalamata olives, pitted and quartered
- 1 tablespoon chopped fresh basil
- 1 tablespoon chopped fresh flat-leaf parsley
- 2 cloves garlic, minced
- 4 8-ounce boneless, skinless chicken breasts
- ¼ teaspoon salt
- ½ teaspoon ground pepper
- 1 tablespoon extra-virgin olive oil
- 1 tablespoon lemon juice

1. Preheat oven to 400°F. Combine feta, roasted red peppers, spinach, olives, basil, parsley and garlic in a medium bowl.

2. Using a small knife, cut a horizontal slit through the thickest portion of each chicken breast to form a pocket. Stuff each breast pocket with about ⅓ cup of the feta mixture; secure the pockets using wooden picks. Sprinkle the chicken evenly with salt and pepper.

3. Heat oil in a large oven-safe skillet over medium-high heat. Arrange the stuffed breasts, top-sides down, in the pan; cook until golden, about 2 minutes. Carefully flip the chicken; transfer the pan to the oven. Bake until an instant-read thermometer inserted in the thickest portion of the chicken registers 165°F, 20 to 25 minutes. Drizzle the chicken evenly with lemon juice. Remove the wooden picks from the chicken before serving.

SERVES 8: ½ BREAST EACH
CAL 179 **FAT** 7G (SAT 3G) **CHOL** 71MG **CARBS** 2G
TOTAL SUGARS 1G (ADDED 0G) **PROTEIN** 24G **FIBER** 0G
SODIUM 352MG **POTASSIUM** 213MG

Pan-Seared Halibut with Creamed Corn & Tomatoes

ACTIVE: 40 min **TOTAL:** 40 min

This recipe calls for halibut—line-caught from the Pacific Ocean is the most sustainable option. Can't find it? Swap in Pacific cod or U.S. farmed tilapia instead.

- **4 ears corn, husked**
- **1½ cups whole milk**
- **3 cloves garlic, divided**
- **1 sprig fresh thyme**
- **3 cups chopped tomatoes**
- **3 tablespoons chopped fresh basil**
- **2 tablespoons extra-virgin olive oil, divided**
- **¾ teaspoon salt, divided**
- **1 tablespoon butter**
- **¼ cup chopped shallot**
- **2 tablespoons all-purpose flour**
- **2 tablespoons grated Parmesan cheese**
- **½ teaspoon ground pepper, divided**
- **1¼ pounds halibut, cut into 4 portions**

1. Cut kernels from cobs and set aside. Cut or break the cobs in half and place in a large saucepan. Add milk, 2 garlic cloves and thyme. Cook over medium heat until starting to simmer around the edges. Remove from heat, cover and let steep for 10 minutes. Strain into a glass measuring cup or small bowl; discard the solids.

2. Meanwhile, grate the remaining garlic clove into a medium bowl. Stir in tomatoes, basil, 1 tablespoon oil and ¼ teaspoon salt. Set aside.

3. Melt butter in the pan over medium heat. Add shallots and cook, stirring occasionally, until soft, about 1 minute. Add the reserved corn kernels and cook, stirring occasionally, until starting to soften, about 3 minutes. Sprinkle with flour and cook for 30 seconds. While stirring, slowly add the milk. Adjust heat to maintain a simmer, cover and cook until thickened, about 5 minutes. Stir in Parmesan and ¼ teaspoon each salt and pepper. Cover and set aside.

4. Sprinkle halibut with the remaining ¼ teaspoon each salt and pepper. Heat the remaining 1 tablespoon oil in a large nonstick skillet over medium-high heat. Add the halibut and cook, turning once, until lightly browned and just cooked through, 5 to 7 minutes total.

5. Serve the halibut with the reserved creamed corn and tomatoes.

SERVES 4: 4 OZ. HALIBUT & ½ CUP EACH CORN & TOMATOES
CAL 422 **FAT** 17G (SAT 6G) **CHOL** 88MG **CARBS** 35G
TOTAL SUGARS 15G (ADDED 0G) **PROTEIN** 35G
FIBER 4G **SODIUM** 641MG **POTASSIUM** 1,396MG

Chicken Pita Sandwiches with Harissa Sauce

ACTIVE: 35 min **TOTAL:** 4 hr 35 min
EQUIPMENT: 6-qt. or larger slow cooker

We tuck this lemon-oregano chicken into pitas with lots of fixings, but you could ditch the pita and serve it all over cooked bulgur, cauliflower rice or a bed of greens.

- Zest and juice of 1 lemon
- 1 tablespoon ground cumin
- 1 tablespoon dried oregano
- 3 teaspoons grated garlic, divided
- ½ teaspoon ground allspice
- ½ teaspoon kosher salt, divided
- ½ teaspoon ground pepper, divided
- 3 pounds boneless, skinless chicken thighs, trimmed
- 6 tablespoons tahini
- ¼ cup water
- 2 tablespoons harissa paste
- 8 whole-wheat pitas, warmed if desired
- Shredded romaine, diced tomatoes and slivered red onion, for serving

1. Combine lemon zest and juice, cumin, oregano, 2 teaspoons garlic, allspice and ¼ teaspoon each salt and pepper in a 6-quart or larger slow cooker. Add chicken and toss to coat. Cook on Low for 4 hours.

2. Meanwhile, whisk tahini, water, harissa, the remaining 1 teaspoon garlic and ⅛ teaspoon each salt and pepper in a small bowl. Refrigerate until ready to serve.

3. Transfer the chicken to a clean cutting board and let rest for 5 minutes. Shred the chicken and toss in a bowl with ¼ cup of the juices from the slow cooker and the remaining ⅛ teaspoon each salt and pepper. Serve the chicken in pitas with the sauce and lettuce, tomato and onion, if desired.

SERVES 8: 1 PITA SANDWICH EACH
CAL 530 **FAT** 20G (SAT 4G) **CHOL** 113MG
CARBS 49G **TOTAL SUGARS** 3G (ADDED 0G)
PROTEIN 41G **FIBER** 6G **SODIUM** 670MG
POTASSIUM 432MG

Green Shakshuka with Spinach, Chard & Feta

ACTIVE: 30 min **TOTAL:** 30 min

The inspiration for this green shakshuka recipe comes from HaBasta, a popular restaurant on the edge of Carmel Market in Tel Aviv, where the shakshuka is packed with green chard and spinach, and a little hot pepper provides just a touch of spice. Serve with pita or crusty bread to sop up the sauce for a quick dinner or for brunch.

- ⅓ cup extra-virgin olive oil
- 1 large onion, finely chopped
- 12 ounces chard, stemmed and chopped
- 12 ounces mature spinach, stemmed and chopped
- ½ cup dry white wine
- 1 small jalapeño *or* serrano pepper, thinly sliced
- 2 medium cloves garlic, very thinly sliced
- ¼ teaspoon kosher salt
- ¼ teaspoon ground pepper
- ½ cup low-sodium no-chicken *or* chicken broth
- 2 tablespoons unsalted butter
- 6 large eggs
- ½ cup crumbled feta *or* goat cheese

1. Heat oil in a large skillet over medium heat. Add onion and cook, stirring often, until soft and translucent but not browned, 7 to 8 minutes. Add chard and spinach, a few handfuls at a time, and cook, stirring often, until wilted, about 5 minutes. Add wine, jalapeño (or serrano), garlic, salt and pepper; cook, stirring occasionally, until the wine is absorbed and the garlic softens, 2 to 4 minutes. Add broth and butter; cook, stirring, until the butter is melted and some of the liquid is absorbed, 1 to 2 minutes.

2. Crack eggs over the vegetables. Cover and cook over medium-low heat until the whites are set, 3 to 5 minutes. Remove from heat and sprinkle with cheese; cover and let stand for 2 minutes before serving.

SERVES 6: 1 EGG & ½ CUP GREENS EACH
CAL 296 **FAT** 23G (SAT 7G) **CHOL** 205MG **CARBS** 8G
TOTAL SUGARS 3G (ADDED 0G) **PROTEIN** 11G **FIBER** 3G
SODIUM 418MG **POTASSIUM** 669MG

Prosciutto Pizza with Corn & Arugula

ACTIVE: 20 min **TOTAL:** 20 min

Prosciutto and arugula elevate this simple grilled pizza. If you have time, let the dough stand at room temperature for 10 to 15 minutes to make rolling it out easier. Thawed frozen corn works in place of fresh—just pat it dry before sprinkling it on the pizza.

- **1 pound pizza dough, preferably whole-wheat**
- **2 tablespoons extra-virgin olive oil, divided**
- **1 clove garlic, minced**
- **1 cup part-skim shredded mozzarella cheese**
- **1 cup fresh corn kernels**
- **1 ounce very thinly sliced prosciutto, torn into 1-inch pieces**
- **1½ cups arugula**
- **½ cup torn fresh basil**
- **¼ teaspoon ground pepper**

1. Preheat grill to medium-high.
2. Roll dough out on a lightly floured surface into a 12-inch oval. Transfer to a lightly floured large baking sheet. Combine 1 tablespoon oil and garlic in a small bowl. Bring the dough, the garlic oil, cheese, corn and prosciutto to the grill.
3. Oil the grill rack. Transfer the crust to the grill. Grill the dough until puffed and lightly browned, 1 to 2 minutes.
4. Flip the crust over and spread the garlic oil on it. Top with the cheese, corn and prosciutto. Grill, covered, until the cheese is melted and the crust is lightly browned on the bottom, 2 to 3 minutes more. Return the pizza to the baking sheet.
5. Top the pizza with arugula, basil and pepper. Drizzle with the remaining 1 tablespoon oil.

SERVES 4: ¼ PIZZA EACH
CAL 436 **FAT** 20G (SAT 5G) **CHOL** 24MG
CARBS 53G **TOTAL SUGARS** 5G (ADDED 1G)
PROTEIN 18G **FIBER** 3G **SODIUM** 684MG
POTASSIUM 199MG

Slow-Cooker Mediterranean Chicken & Chickpea Soup

ACTIVE: 20 min **TOTAL:** 4 hrs 20 min
EQUIPMENT: 6-qt. or larger slow cooker

This set-it-and-forget-it slow-cooker recipe simmers away all day so you come home to a warm and healthy dinner the whole family will love. Using bone-in chicken is the key to making rich soup without adding broth.

1½ cups dried chickpeas, soaked overnight
4 cups water
1 large yellow onion, finely chopped
1 15-ounce can no-salt-added diced tomatoes, preferably fire-roasted
2 tablespoons tomato paste
4 cloves garlic, finely chopped
1 bay leaf
4 teaspoons ground cumin
4 teaspoons paprika
¼ teaspoon cayenne pepper
¼ teaspoon ground pepper
2 pounds bone-in chicken thighs, skin removed, trimmed
1 14-ounce can artichoke hearts, drained and quartered
¼ cup halved pitted oil-cured olives
½ teaspoon salt
¼ cup chopped fresh parsley or cilantro

1. Drain chickpeas and place in a 6-quart or larger slow cooker. Add 4 cups water, onion, tomatoes and their juice, tomato paste, garlic, bay leaf, cumin, paprika, cayenne and ground pepper; stir to combine. Add chicken.

2. Cover and cook on Low for 8 hours or High for 4 hours.

3. Transfer the chicken to a clean cutting board and let cool slightly. Discard bay leaf. Add artichokes, olives and salt to the slow cooker and stir to combine. Shred the chicken, discarding bones. Stir the chicken into the soup. Serve topped with parsley (or cilantro).

SERVES 6: ABOUT 2 CUPS EACH
CAL 447 **FAT** 15G (SAT 3G) **CHOL** 77MG **CARBS** 43G
TOTAL SUGARS 9G (ADDED 0G) **PROTEIN** 34G **FIBER** 12G
SODIUM 762MG **POTASSIUM** 609MG

Slow-Cooker Mediterranean Stew

ACTIVE: 15 mins **TOTAL:** 6 hrs 45 min

This Mediterranean stew is a healthy dinner chock-full of vegetables and hearty chickpeas. A drizzle of olive oil to finish carries the flavors. Swap out the chickpeas for white beans for a different twist, or try collards or spinach in place of the kale.

- 2 14-ounce cans no-salt-added fire-roasted diced tomatoes
- 3 cups low-sodium vegetable broth
- 1 cup coarsely chopped onion
- ¾ cup chopped carrot
- 4 cloves garlic, minced
- 1 teaspoon dried oregano
- ¾ teaspoon salt
- ½ teaspoon crushed red pepper
- ¼ teaspoon ground pepper
- 1 15-ounce can no-salt-added chickpeas, rinsed, divided
- 1 bunch lacinato kale, stemmed and chopped (about 8 cups)
- 1 tablespoon lemon juice
- 3 tablespoons extra-virgin olive oil
- 8 leaves fresh basil, torn if large
- 6 lemon wedges, for serving

1. Combine tomatoes, broth, onion, carrot, garlic, oregano, salt, crushed red pepper and pepper in a 4-quart slow cooker. Cover and cook on Low for 6 hours.

2. Measure ¼ cup of the cooking liquid from the slow cooker into a small bowl. Add 2 tablespoons chickpeas; mash with a fork until smooth.

3. Add the mashed chickpeas, kale, lemon juice and remaining whole chickpeas to the mixture in the slow cooker. Stir to combine. Cover and cook on Low until the kale is tender, about 30 minutes.

4. Ladle the stew evenly into 6 bowls; drizzle with oil. Garnish with basil. Serve with lemon wedges, if desired.

SERVES 6: 1¾ CUPS EACH
CAL 191 **FAT** 8G (SAT 1G) **CHOL** 0G **CARBS** 23G
TOTAL SUGARS 7G (ADDED 0G) **PROTEIN** 6G **FIBER** 6G
SODIUM 416MG **POTASSIUM** 310MG

Salmon Cakes with Arugula Salad

ACTIVE: 35 min **TOTAL:** 35 min

After making the salmon cakes, we firm them up for 5 minutes in the freezer before cooking so they don't fall apart when they hit the hot oil.

- **1 pound salmon, preferably wild, skinned**
- **2 tablespoons lemon juice, divided**
- **2 teaspoons Dijon mustard, divided**
- **½ cup finely chopped yellow bell pepper**
- **1 tablespoon finely chopped shallot**
- **½ teaspoon ground pepper, divided**
- **½ cup panko breadcrumbs**
- **½ cup crème fraîche *or* sour cream**
- **¼ cup buttermilk**
- **3 tablespoons chopped fresh dill**
- **½ teaspoon extra-virgin olive oil**
- **1 5-ounce package arugula**
- **1 cup sliced radishes**

1. Coarsely chop salmon and place half in a food processor. Add 1 tablespoon lemon juice and 1 teaspoon mustard. Process, scraping down the sides as necessary, until smooth. Add the remaining salmon, bell pepper, shallot and ¼ teaspoon pepper and pulse until the mixture is combined but still chunky.

2. Transfer the salmon mixture to a medium bowl. Add breadcrumbs and stir until combined. Form the salmon into 4 patties, about 4 inches wide each, and place on a plate. Freeze for 5 minutes.

3. Meanwhile, whisk crème fraîche (or sour cream), buttermilk, dill and ¼ teaspoon salt with the remaining 1 tablespoon lemon juice, 1 teaspoon mustard and ¼ teaspoon pepper in a large bowl. Set aside ¼ cup of the dressing for drizzling.

4. Heat oil in a large cast-iron or nonstick skillet over medium-high heat. Add the salmon cakes and cook, flipping once, until well browned and cooked through, 2 to 3 minutes per side. Transfer to a clean plate and sprinkle with the remaining ¼ teaspoon salt.

5. Add arugula and radishes to the dressing in the large bowl. Toss to coat. Serve the salmon cakes on top of the salad, drizzled with the reserved ¼ cup dressing.

SERVES 4: 1 SALMON PATTY & 1½ CUPS SALAD EACH
CAL 424 **FAT** 27G (SAT 9G) **CHOL** 97MG **CARBS** 14G
TOTAL SUGARS 4G (ADDED 0G) **PROTEIN** 30G **FIBER** 2G
SODIUM 494MG **POTASSIUM** 923MG

Walnut-Rosemary Crusted Salmon

ACTIVE: 10 min **TOTAL:** 20 min

Salmon and walnuts are both great sources of omega-3 fatty acids. Pair this easy salmon recipe with a simple salad and a side of roasted potatoes or quinoa.

- 2 teaspoons Dijon mustard
- 1 clove garlic, minced
- ¼ teaspoon lemon zest
- 1 teaspoon lemon juice
- 1 teaspoon chopped fresh rosemary
- ½ teaspoon honey
- ½ teaspoon kosher salt
- ¼ teaspoon crushed red pepper
- 3 tablespoons panko breadcrumbs
- 3 tablespoons finely chopped walnuts
- 1 teaspoon extra-virgin olive oil
- 1 1-pound skinless salmon fillet, fresh or frozen
- Olive oil cooking spray
- Chopped fresh parsley and lemon wedges for garnish

1. Preheat oven to 425°F. Line a large rimmed baking sheet with parchment paper.
2. Combine mustard, garlic, lemon zest, lemon juice, rosemary, honey, salt and crushed red pepper in a small bowl. Combine panko, walnuts and oil in another small bowl.
3. Place salmon on the prepared baking sheet. Spread the mustard mixture over the fish and sprinkle with the panko mixture, pressing to adhere. Lightly coat with cooking spray.
4. Bake until the fish flakes easily with a fork, 8 to 12 minutes, depending on thickness.
5. Sprinkle with parsley and serve with lemon wedges, if desired.

SERVES 4: 3 OUNCES EACH
CAL 222 **FAT** 12G (SAT 2G) **CHOL** 62 **CARBS** 4G
TOTAL SUGARS 1G (ADDED 1G) **PROTEIN** 24G **FIBER** 0G
SODIUM 256MG

Editor-In-Chief Jessie Price
Creative Director James Van Fleteren

Mediterranean Diet

Editorial Director Kostya Kennedy
Creative Director Gary Stewart
Editor Courtney Mifsud
Art Director Ronnie Brandwein-Keats
Photo Editor Rachel Hatch
Writers Jessica Ball, Jane Black, Helen Ellis, Sunny Sea Gold, Paul Greenberg, Joyce Hendley, Emily Joshu, Aglaia Kremezi, Hallie Levine, Melinda Wenner Moyer, Holly Pevzner, Jen Rose Smith, Christina Vercelletto, Jamie Vespa, Korsha Wilson
Copy Editor Ben Ake
Reporter Ryan Hatch
Production Designer Sandra Jurevics
Premedia Trafficking Supervisor Paige E. King
Color Quality Analyst John Santucci

MEREDITH PREMIUM PUBLISHING
Vice President & Group Publisher Scott Mortimer
Vice President, Group Editorial Director Stephen Orr
Vice President, Marketing Jeremy Biloon
Director, Brand Marketing Jean Kennedy
Associate Director, Brand Marketing Bryan Christian
Senior Brand Manager Katherine Barnet

Editorial Director Kostya Kennedy
Creative Director Gary Stewart
Director of Photography Christina Lieberman
Editorial Operations Director Jamie Roth Major
Manager, Editorial Operations Gina Scauzillo

Special thanks Brad Beatson, Samantha Lebofsky, Kate Roncinske, Joel Van Liew, Laura Villano

MEREDITH NATIONAL MEDIA GROUP
President, Meredith Magazines Doug Olson
President, Consumer Products Tom Witschi
President, Chief Digital Officer Catherine Levene
Chief Business & Data Officer Alysia Borsa
Chief Revenue Officer Michael Brownstein
Marketing & Integrated Communications Nancy Weber

SENIOR VICE PRESIDENTS
Consumer Revenue Andy Wilson
Corporate Sales Brian Kightlinger
Research Solutions Britta Cleveland
Strategic Sourcing, Newsstand, Production Chuck Howell
Digital Sales Marla Newman
The Foundry Matt Petersen
Product & Technology Justin Law

VICE PRESIDENTS
Finance Chris Susil
Business Planning & Analysis Rob Silverstone
Consumer Marketing Steve Crowe
Brand Licensing Toye Cody and Sondra Newkirk
Corporate Communications Jill Davison
Vice President, Group Editorial Director Stephen Orr
Director, Editorial Operations & Finance Greg Kayko

MEREDITH CORPORATION
Chairman & Chief Executive Officer Tom Harty
Chief Financial Officer Jason Frierott
Chief Development Officer John Zieser
Chief Strategy Officer Daphne Kwon
President, Meredith Local Media Group Patrick McCreery
Senior Vice President, Human Resources Dina Nathanson

Vice Chairman Mell Meredith Frazier

Printed in the USA.

Photo Credits

FRONT COVER
sveta_zarzamora/iStock/Getty Images

BACK COVER
(Clockwise from top) Floriana/E+/Getty Images; Kang Kim/Offset; Enrique Diaz/7cero/Moment RF/Getty Images

TITLE PAGE
Pixel Stories/Stocksy

CONTENTS
humanmade/iStock/Getty Images

INTRODUCTION
P. 4 (icons, from left) Aliaksei_7799/iStock/Getty Images (2); oleg7799/iStock/Getty Images
P. 5 losangela/Adobe Stock
P. 6 Anchiy/E+/Getty Images

PP. 8, 9 Eva Katalin Kondoros/E+/Getty Images
P. 11 Bonninstudio/Stocksy
PP. 12, 13 Foxys_forest_manufacture/iStock/Getty Images
P. 15 Dolphia Nandi/Stocksy
P. 16 Westphalen Photography Inc.
P. 19 Canan Czemmel/Westend61/Offset
P. 21 Foxys_forest_manufacture/iStock/Getty Images
P. 22 Gligatron/iStock/Getty Images
P. 25 Dan Cretu/Moment Open/Getty Images
P. 27 Photograph by Matthew Roharik. Styling by Jessica Stewart
P. 28 Alex Taranukhin/Adobe Stock
P. 30 Erin Kunkel
P. 33 Trinette Reed/Stocksy
P. 35 Borislav Zhuykov/Stocksy
P. 36 zeljkosantrac/E+/Getty Images
PP. 38, 39 Alexey Oblov/Moment RF/Getty Images
PP. 40, 41 Stefan Deutsch/Westend61/Offset
P. 42 milangonda/Cavan Images
P. 43 Illustration by Heather Gatley
P. 45 Leigh Beisch
PP. 46, 47 Design Pics Inc./National Geographic
P. 48 Robert Harding Picture Library/National Geographic
PP. 50–53 Leigh Beisch (3)
P. 54 rawf8/Shutterstock
P. 55 SolStock/E+/Getty Images
P. 57 Penny De Los Santos
P. 58 Illustration by Heather Gatley
PP. 59–61 Penny De Los Santos (2)
PP. 62–65 Marco Di Lauro/Getty Images (4)
PP. 66, 67 Penny De Los Santos (2)
PP. 68, 69 Alba Vitta/Offset
P. 71 Xsandra/E+/Getty Images
P. 72 nicknick_ko/Adobe Stock
P. 73 Joern Rynio/Stocksy
PP. 74, 75 Alexander Spatari/Moment RF/Getty Images
PP. 76, 77 Cavan Images/Getty Images
P. 79 Juan Moyano/Stocksy
PP. 80, 81 Brie Passano
PP. 82–84 Blaine Moats (3)
P. 85 Marty Baldwin
P. 86 Greg DuPree
PP. 87, 88 Blaine Moats (2)
P. 89 Penny De Los Santos
P. 90 Blaine Moats
P. 91 Jacob Fox
P. 92 Greg DuPree
PP. 93, 94 Blaine Moats (2)
P. 96 Melissa Milis Photography/Stocksy

Savor Every Bite

Eating like a Mediterranean is as much lifestyle as it is diet. Instead of gobbling your meal in front of the TV, slow down and sit down at the table with your family and friends to savor what you're eating. Not only will you enjoy your company and your food, but eating slowly also allows you to tune in to your body's hunger and fullness signals. You're more apt to eat just until you're satisfied than until you're busting-at-the-seams full. —Jessica Migala

Made in the USA
Coppell, TX
30 November 2023